FOOTSTEPS
in the CLOUDS

FOOTSTEPS
in the CLOUDS

Kangchenjunga
A Century Later

Baiba & Pat Morrow

First published in 1999 by

Raincoast Books
8680 Cambie Street
Vancouver, B.C.
V6P 6M9
(604) 323-7100

www.raincoast.com

1   2   3   4   5   6   7   8   9   10

CANADIAN CATALOGUING IN PUBLICATION DATA

Morrow, Baiba
    Footsteps in the clouds

    (Raincoast journeys)
    ISBN 1-55192-226-6

    1.   Morrow, Baiba – Journeys – Kanchenjunga (Nepal and India) 2. Morrow, Pat – Journeys – Kanchenjunga
    (Nepal and India) 3. Mountaineering – Kanchenjunga (Nepal and India) 4. Kanchenjunga (Nepal and India)—
    Description and travel. 5. Kanchenjunga (Nepal and India) – Pictorial works. I. Morrow, Pat. II. Title. III.
    Series.
        GV199.44.K36M67   1999   796.52'2'095496   C99-910498-5

Editing by Andrew Nikiforuk
Text and cover design by Val Speidel
Colour Separations by Chromatech Inc., Vancouver, B.C., Canada

The Canada Council | Le Conseil des Arts
FOR THE ARTS | DU CANADA
SINCE 1957 | DEPUIS 1957

Printed in Italy

Raincoast Books gratefully acknowledges the support of the Government of Canada, through the Book Publishing Industry Development Program, the Canada Council and the Department of Canadian Heritage. We also acknowledge the assistance of the Province of British Columbia, through the British Columbia Arts Council.

For the hill people of Nepal and Sikkim, who give of themselves so freely

Contents

PAGES II–III. *The eastern foothills of Nepal, seen from the pass of Mirgin La, spread out to the south of Kangchenjunga like waves of an ocean.*

PAGE VI. *Dave Quinn climbs up the icy slopes of Drohma Peak, above our camp at Pangpema, to get a better view of Kangchenjunga's formidable north face.*

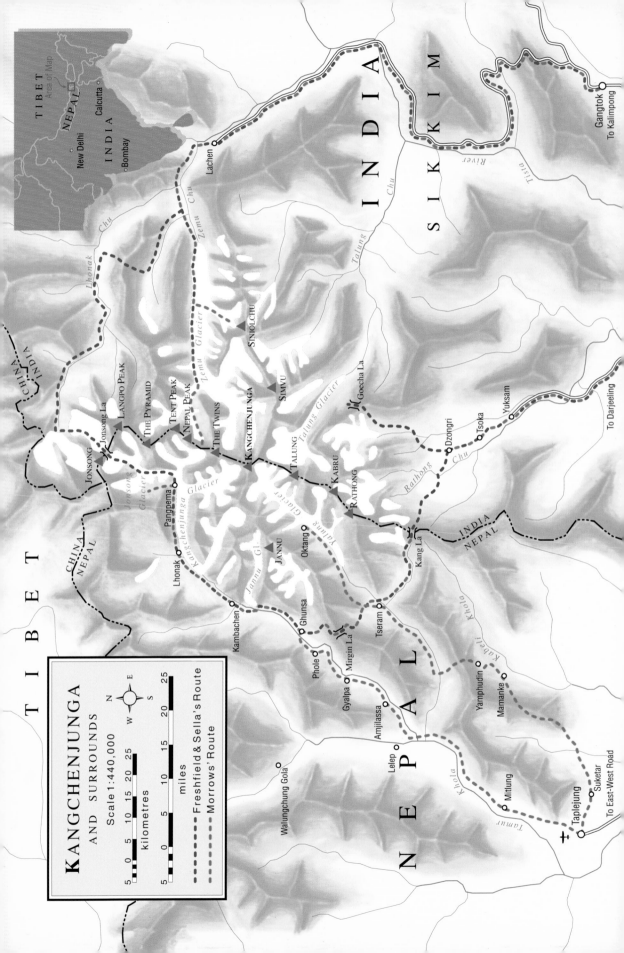

INTRODUCTION

Do not follow in the footsteps of the men of old. Seek, instead, what they sought.

—Basho

I N 1995 MY HUSBAND, PAT MORROW, SAT ON THE JURY FOR ROBERT Schauer's annual "Mountain & Adventure Film Festival" in Graz, Austria. There he met Paul Kallmes, an entrepreneur and climber from Massachusetts. Paul's interest in the work of the world's greatest pioneer mountain photographer, Vittorio Sella, had developed into a passion. He had come to launch a photographic exhibit of the the 19th century master craftsman.

Long a fan of Sella, Pat could not take his eyes off Sella's exquisite large-format, black and white portraits of the world's third highest mountain – Kangchenjunga.

Over numerous beers Pat and Paul soon discovered a common interest in both Sella and the seasoned British climber and explorer, Douglas Freshfield. In 1899 the two men made history by circumnavigating Kangchenjunga, which straddled the then-forbidden enclave of Nepal and the Buddhist kingdom of Sikkim.

Their trek took seven grueling weeks. For protection against aggressive brigands and xenophobic Tibetan guards patrolling the high passes of Sikkim's northern frontier, the 54 year-old Englishman wisely hired six armed Gurkhas. Once on the mountain's west side, the expedition traveled clandestinely. In those days the British Raj honored Nepal's closed door policy and Freshfield did not want to risk an international incident.

Italian photographer Vittorio Sella (1859–1943)

The expedition also battled a fierce storm. After two meters of snow fell in as many days in the Zemu Valley the explorers nearly turned around. But Freshfield rallied his teammates and diverted their route over Jonsong La. At 6145 meters this pass is nearly as high as Denali (Mount McKinley), North America's highest peak.

After completing the circle around Kangchenjunga, the team returned to Darjeeling, well weathered yet triumphant. The subsequent combination of Sella's hallmark photographs and Freshfield's skilled narrative made *Round Kangchenjunga* an instant classic in Himalayan annals.

Although now dwarfed by Everest's height and fame, Kangchenjunga was once the most famous of all Himalayan peaks, and deservedly so. Its snowy form dominates the view from Darjeeling, India's popular hill resort, and anchors the eastern wing of the Himalaya like a celestial bookend. Until 1849 it was thought to be the world's highest mountain.

Of all fourteen 8000-meter peaks in the Himalaya, Kangchenjunga remains the holiest. Its Tibetan name means "The Five Treasuries of Eternal Snow," referring to the five summits that make up the massif. In each summit lies hidden one of the treasures of prosperity: gold, silver, gems, grains and holy books. To the people who live in its shadow Kangchenjunga remains home to the region's protective deity. And to the Lepchas, the aboriginal residents of Sikkim, the mountain god not only created the very first man and woman on earth but still carefully watches over the tiny state to ensure its welfare.

For Freshfield, a president of both the prestigious Alpine Club and Royal Geographical Society, the girdling of this snowy 8595-meter-high peak was the culmination of a remarkable mountain career. And for the inventive Sella, the son of a textile manufacturer in Biella, Italy, the journey was a marvelous opportunity to bring back virgin images of the wildest Himalaya.

Inspired by Sella's photographs, Pat and Paul proposed a journey commemorating the 1899 expedition. In addition they also conspired to climb one of Kangchenjunga's lovely satellite peaks, Mount Siniolchu. Described by Freshfield as "the most superb triumph of mountain architecture" and photographed by Sella with obvious reverence, the pristine peak held strong aesthetic appeal.

Structured along the pyramidal lines of Europe's Matterhorn or Peru's Alpamayo, Siniolchu is a symmetrical spear of snow and ice that pierces the sky at 6887 meters.

Douglas Freshfield (1845–1934) was described upon his death by a British contemporary as a "great and very perfect gentleman, and a peerless mountain explorer."

Almost completely unknown outside of Sikkim, the peak has only been climbed five times.

As we set about planning the logistics for our trip, we knew that a true circumnavigation à la Freshfield was no longer possible. Protocol to visit the area has actually become more difficult than it was a century ago. Where the British and Russian empires once schemed, India, China and Pakistan now jostle for power.

Not wanting to cause an international border incident (and not relishing the thought of being shot at by the trigger-happy Indo-Tibetan Border Police), we decided to break our 1998 circle of the mountain into two treks. The first leg took us from Sikkim to Kangchenjunga's northeastern flanks with an attempt on Siniolchu and ended at the high pass of Nepal Gap. For the second half we explored Nepal's side of the mountain up the Tamur River. To complete our circle we returned to Sikkim and walked to Dzongri, a high alpine pasture couched on Kangchenjunga's southern flanks.

In the end, Freshfield and Sella were not our only mentors. In the last century Sikkim's immense charms attracted an eclectic roster of European mountaineers, mystics, artists, and social misfits. They included Alexandra David-Neel, a bold French adventuress and Buddhist scholar, Aleister Crowley, the possibly most lecherous man to ever scale a mountain, and Nicholas Roerich, a celebrated Russian artist and philosopher. Each rubbed shoulders with Darjeeling's British gentry at hotels like the stately Windamere before striking off through the virgin forests of Sikkim. We wanted to explore their legacy, too.

Like most great journeys into wild mountains Freshfield's expedition began with a simple and sublime invitation to Sella. After the two men explored Russia's Caucasus Mountains together Freshfield scribbled a postcard to his friend and casually suggested another trek, this time to the distant Himalaya.

"I am an uncertain person balancing possibilities," Freshfield wrote to Sella. "Could I hope to get you to bring your equipment and experience? I am very lazy and inefficient in making elaborate preparations. Still it just might be worth our while to turn it over in our minds as an idea…. I should like to see those great peaks and to go round Kangchenjunga."

A century later, we took this to be our invitation as well.

Chapter 1

RUSH HOUR IN SHANGRI-LA

Darjeeling, India, April 24, 1998

EARLY IN THE MORNING PAT AND I FELL IN LINE WITH THE locals walking clockwise around Observatory Hill in the old colonial tea town of Darjeeling. While the devout spun their prayer wheels in dizzying rotations and mantras hung in the air like clouds, we waited for the sun to illuminate Kangchenjunga. As everyone in Darjeeling knows, "the Hill" offers one of the best panoramic views of the Himalaya in all of India.

Although we doubted we would be blessed with a clear sunrise, the walk was a welcome relief after yesterday's bumpy bus ride from Bagdogra on the northern Indian plains. As we rounded the Hill at 6:00 A.M. the clouds gently parted. The locals turned and bowed their heads with hands clasped in prayer. Kangchenjunga, their sacred guardian, now commanded everyone's attention like some ancient giant Buddha. As the mountain filled the sky with its immense beauty, I, too, felt compelled to offer my prayers – or something – in reverence. Overawed, all I could muster was a hushed, "Wow."

Like thousands of visitors before us, we grappled for words to describe this heavenly vision. The British climber Frank Smythe found himself in a similar

Darjeeling, established by the British as a hill resort and tea plantation in 1848, still attracts tourists for its unrivalled view of Kangchenjunga, just 75 kilometers away.

7

predicament more than 50 years ago and wrote much about the mountain's surreal power over heart and soul:

> The most rationally minded of men cannot gaze from Darjeeling upon Kangchen-junga without experiencing something of the same emotions of the simpler-minded Sherpas and Lepchas who dwell in the valleys below. He will find himself wondering half in shame if there is anything in the tales told him of the powerful god whose sacred throne rests upon its summits ... and whether the snow-fields and glaciers suspended in mid-air above a misty ocean are indeed abiding places of the Mi-go, the Abominable Snow Men.

Tourist literature identifies Shangri-Las all over the Himalaya, but ancient Tibetan texts suggest a real one lies hidden in the lush folds of Kangchenjunga. According to legend the mountain is home to a *bayul* – a secret valley that harbors peace, happiness and beauty in times of trouble, much like the Shangri-La of James Hilton's novel *Lost Horizon*. After our hellish days in Delhi the idea that we might now be looking at a Shangri-La refreshed my spirit.

Delhi, India, April 20, 1998

Outside Indira Gandhi International Airport a cloying heat immediately smothered Pat and me in a damp gauze of sweat. So, too, did a jostling horde of scrawny-limbed peasants wearing turbans and discolored dhotis. New Delhi may be far from our home in Canmore, Alberta, but at two in the morning after a series of long flights, it seemed equally distant from our destination: the snowy peaks of Sikkim.

"Which way to the Himalaya?" I felt like shouting to the unlikely mob. But dark eyes, conditioned by the surety of fate, stared vacantly, offering no reply. I knew the way anyway: turn left outside the airport and then go east for a thousand kilometers. There we would find Kangchenjunga, our mecca of snow and ice, amid deep green forests.

We pushed through dozens of ragged, sleeping bodies sprawled on the bald pavement and walked into the dark poverty that is India.

After months of planning and last minute uncertainties, our arrival in Delhi felt like a major accomplishment. But neither Pat nor I was celebrating yet. We still lacked the necessary permit to climb Siniolchu. This formidable icy pyramid lies in a restricted area on the east side of Kangchenjunga near the Tibetan border. Final pre-departure faxes from the Indian Mountaineering Foundation (IMF), a sort of mountain-guarding bureaucracy attached to the Ministry of Home Affairs, had assured us that all would be in order upon our arrival.

Knowing full well the capacity of India's head-wagging bureaucrats to turn climbing expeditions into paper chases we had serious doubts. Our expedition had already been postponed in the autumn of 1997 when the IMF abruptly withdrew our permit a month before our departure.

"Maybe this time one or two of India's 33 million Hindu deities will be on our side," said Pat hopefully.

By "our side" Pat meant our "e-mail-order" team. At the top of the list was Paul Kallmes, the 37-year-old American expedition co-leader. Just three years ago Pat and Paul had come up with the idea of retracing Douglas Freshfield's footsteps around Kangchenjunga.

Ever since then the team had expanded and shrunk with amoeba-like random-ness as friends and acquaintances signed on and out for various reasons. Of those originally invited only Ali Palmer and Ace Kvale, both seasoned mountaineers from Colorado, actually made it to India. Besides Paul, Ace was the only one we knew. He had boyish good looks and a snappy motto: "You're never too old to have a happy childhood." Ace had turned to adventure photography after many years of working as a ski model in Verbier, Switzerland. His photographic skills soon earned him a place on numerous expeditions to Asia, including the Great Trango Tower in Pakistan and Ama Dablam in Nepal.

Ali Palmer, a 36-year-old physiotherapist originally from Britain, came with equally good credentials. She ran her own clinic in Telluride but liked to balance work and play. She had climbed in Peru and Nepal, and had worked as a mountain guide, together with Paul, out of the American Alpine Institute.

Ace's girlfriend, Kit Katzenbach, a fit 28-year-old ski patroller and stone mason, rounded out the expedition team. Although an accomplished rock climber and mountain runner, Kit had never been on a high peak before.

Paul also invited two other Americans for the trek to base camp: John "RJ" Hake, a long-time friend of his from San Francisco, and Leah Rubik, a young public relations agent with one of our sponsors, Malden Mills, the manufacturer of Polartec fabric. Because Leah joined at the last minute, her name did not appear on our permit. This omission would regrettably concern every bureaucrat, big or small, from this point on.

Our motley band of expectant trekkers and climbers emerged sleepily from hotel rooms and met for the first time on the morning of April 20 over breakfast. Having exchanged pleasantries electronically for some time, it was a relief to finally have everyone in the same room.

Paul, a Himalayan rookie, bravely took on the challenge of procuring the team's climbing permit with the gusto of the uninitiated. He began with a determined can-do spirit. Feeling there might be strength in numbers, he proposed that the team "storm the IMF!" Paul strode ahead of us like a general marching into war. We foot soldiers fell in behind.

Finding the IMF, hidden on the outskirts of Delhi, proved to be a mini-expedition by itself. Built in better times, the concrete building houses a mountaineering library, a museum and an outdoor climbing wall that remained conspicuously unoccupied in the 40 degree Celsius heat. The office had plenty of character. Mountains of dog-eared ledgers and files lay stacked in dusty piles. Three ancient Remington typewriters typified the age of the office's technology. Acolytes pecked away in the dim light, hammering each key as hard as their fingers could bear to penetrate three layers of carbon copies. Our file was thick. Everything we had mailed or faxed had been faithfully reproduced by hand, in triplicate. The man commanding this paper empire was Colonel J. P. Bhagatjee.

Three months ago we had duly submitted all necessary permit fees and documentation, complete with 10 passport-sized photos from each member. Yet, we still did not have the necessary clearances. For some inexplicable reason, the Colonel could not pick up the phone and directly ask the Ministry of Home Affairs what had happened to them. Instead, he elected to dictate an official letter, painstakingly recorded on one of the Remingtons. Then he reviewed the document, moving the words around for greater or lesser effect with the stub of a pencil.

We waited, and we waited. The officious delay at least gave us a chance to meet the team's latest addition, our liaison officer. IMF rules state that all mountaineering expeditions must include such an individual, usually some unfit government employee from the lowlands who hates mountains. The Indian government, it would seem, believes that climbers are clearly spies and transgressors dangerous to the nation's security. They must, therefore, be carefully supervised.

Fortunately, we were assigned as our liaison officer Ugen Tsering Bhutia, a gracious 30-year-old aspiring climber from Pelling in western Sikkim. He spoke excellent English and loved his native mountains. Now he earnestly joined our quest for the permit.

When the Colonel finished his letter, he assigned an underling to escort us to the Ministry of Home Affairs, located in a dreary five-story government building in downtown Delhi. We arrived just past noon as a stream of Indian office workers and citizens with untold grievances filed by. A hand-written sign taped to the wall notified us that visiting hours for foreigners were from 10:00 A.M. to 12:00 P.M.

"Nei, nei nei," the unarmed guard chastised us. "You cannot go in." The Colonel's envoy disappeared alone into the building clutching the letter. We moped around in the sweltering heat by the entrance. After a few hours, our patience ran out. The guard took pity on us and allowed Paul and Ugen to seek out the office. They ran up the stairs to the waiting room where our envoy sat slouched, apparently resigned to letting nature take its course. Our letter lay, unattended, on a nearby desk. Paul pressed the official into action and soon came bounding down the stairs with the necessary authorization in his hand.

"Quick. To the Foreigners Registration Office!" shouted Paul. Our fearless leader, sweat building on his forehead, now led another offensive on another group of bureaucrats. We got there just before 5:00 P.M. and hoped that we could find the right office minion before closing time. A group of slovenly dressed air force pilots from Uzbekistan broadcast a certain infectious surliness into the room as they awaited clearances.

Using delicate American diplomatic techniques, otherwise known as bullying, Paul convinced one of the workers of the urgency of our affairs. Time spent chasing permits equaled time subtracted from our expedition. The obliging functionary scrawled a messy note entitled "Observations" in each of our passports. This converted our "tourist" visas into the requisite "X" visas which our Indian embassies back home had refused to issue because we had no proof of the climbing permit. By the time we had finished, it was too late to return to Colonel Bhagatjee. Delhi had us at its mercy for another day.

Next morning the good Colonel informed us that the Ministry of Defense was now demanding that a second liaison officer from the military accompany us. We would, of course, be responsible for his upkeep.

"You mean that after paying the $10,000 permit fee, we still have to pay more?" I blurted out.

"Oh, Madame," he replied with a waggle of his head which in India can mean either yes or no. "We want to help you, but in this matter we must not compromise. You know it would be a shame if you arrived in Gangtok and the Sikkim government saw that you did not have a liaison officer from our army, then you would have more delays." Again, his head moved as if it was attached to loose hinges. "We will make sure that this means only a slight increase in your costs. India is, after all, a democracy."

"Well, where we come from, we'd call this something else," I replied caustically. At that, the colonel threw up his hands in resignation.

While the cost of our permit seemed exorbitant, it was nowhere near the price tag attached to a trophy peak such as Everest. The "Big E," as Pat calls it, now commands a sum of US$70,000 just for the permit. But even that amount pales in comparison with the million dollars paid to the Chinese government by a Japanese team in 1992 for the privilege of climbing Namche Barwa in eastern Tibet, at that time the world's highest unclimbed mountain. As long as climbers are willing to pay, governments will be equally willing to climb into their pockets.

The Colonel now told us to go in person to the Sikkim Home Ministry to collect its official blessing. Paul muttered "Never again" as we turned another corner in the labyrinth set out for us by the government of India. The state seemed to have an unwritten rule of fitness for foreigners: if you can endure the bureaucracy, than you can survive any climb.

At Sikkim House, we were ushered into the lair of an official we quickly dubbed the "Dragon Lady." We arrived unannounced, and our reception was cold. When she finally understood that we were a climbing expedition, she requested all the paperwork. Of course, we did not have it; the Colonel did.

Ugen Tsering retreated to the IMF for the documents. Then the Dragon Lady announced that a US$5,500 bank draft forwarded to her office two months ago was "invalid." It had been made out to the House of Sikkim, as instructed by the IMF, instead of the Resident Commissioner of Sikkim. ("Never again," growled Paul.)

It was now obvious to us that from the very beginning nothing was in order with our permit. It also appeared that our tour operator, Jamling Tenzing, had failed to steer the application through the necessary hoops. Jamling, who starred in the newly released Everest IMAX film, had instead been making guest appearances at the various openings across the United States. Luckily, at the last minute, he had commandeered his cousin's husband to help us in Delhi. Chewang Motup, a Ladakhi with his own Leh-based company called Rimo Tours, now became our saviour in the permit crusade.

When all reason failed, we realized that we would have to make up for the shortfall by pooling our cash. Dollars were unacceptable; payment was to be made in rupees only. Chewang Motup elected to take the cash to his bank in the morning, change it, and then return with the rupees to Sikkim House. After getting a receipt and permit from the Dragon Lady, he promised to give the priceless papers to Ugen who would then catch up with us in Gangtok in a few days. Paul was now repeating his mantra with more fervor than a Tibetan on a holy pilgrimage to Mount Kailas. "Never again, never again, NEVER AGAIN." But at least we could escape the cursed purgatory of Delhi tomorrow.

We collapsed back at our guest house, nursing aching bodies and minds with cold bottles of Kingfisher beer.

"All Freshfield needed was a letter from the King of Sikkim," joked Paul.

"Long live the king!" added Kit.

"Unfortunately, the King is no more." interjected Pat.

The last Chogyal, which means in Tibetan "the king who rules with righteousness," was Palden Thondup Namgyal. He belonged to the dynasty that established Sikkim in the 17th century. The Buddhist kingdom once encompassed not only its present boundaries but eastern Nepal, the Chumbi Valley in Tibet, the Ha Valley in Bhutan, and the foothills of Darjeeling.

After the British withdrew in 1947, the newly independent federation of India began to covet Sikkim's strategic position as a buffer between Tibet, China, Bhutan and Nepal. For centuries the most important and direct trade routes between India and Tibet cut through Sikkim's mountain passes on the southeast border. Natu La (3310 meters) and Jelep La (4374 meters) are relatively low for Himalayan passes and thus easily crossed. India regarded the routes as troublesome points of entry that could be used by its enemy, namely China. In short order Sikkim became a Protectorate of India under a special treaty.

Most of the world had never heard of Sikkim until Chogyal Palden Thondup Namgyal made international headlines in 1963 by marrying Hope Cooke, an American journalist. (Namgyal's first wife, a beautiful Tibetan princess named Sangey Deki, died in 1957.) The fairy tale wedding attracted the attention of journalists who flocked to a kingdom missing from most maps. As the new Queen, Cooke helped put Sikkim on the map.

But Cooke didn't stay long in the fabled Himalayan kingdom. After a wave of unrest gripped the capital in 1973 and the Indian government put the royal family under house arrest, Cooke abruptly left Sikkim and her husband, taking their two children to the U.S. The Chogyal faced increasing pressures from big-brother India as well as from a grass-roots movement vying for a popular government. Two years later India invaded and made Sikkim its 22nd state. Stripped of his powers the last king of Sikkim left the Himalaya and died of cancer in near-obscurity in New York City in 1982.

"May the King rest in peace," I thought. Almost every stronghold of Tibetan Buddhism has now become a conquered entity. India has swallowed Ladakh and Sikkim, while Nepal has absorbed Mustang. The Chinese, of course, have walked all over Tibet. Now Bhutan remains the only independent Buddhist kingdom in the Himalayan region.

The next morning our expedition gladly boarded the plane to Bagdogra, the closest airport to Darjeeling and Gangtok. We slumped into our seats, sweating like cold drinks. Kit, the powerful stone mason, moaned in misery.

"It was yesterday's Eggplant Vegetable Delight at Sikkim House. I think the Dragon Lady was trying to poison me," whimpered our first victim of "Delhi Belly."

The plane headed east into the huge bulwark of thick clouds that muffled the Himalaya. As the air conditioning kicked in, I dreamed of cool mountain air surging through my lungs.

Darjeeling

On our first morning in Darjeeling, all that bureaucratic paper chase seemed a continent away, obliterated by the vista of Kangchenjunga before us. Minutes later, my reverie subsided, as the dawn's rosy glow dissolved into deadened whiteness. The sky darkened and a veil of clouds drifted in again. The heavenly vision was gone but its impact lingered. We walked back to the Sherpa International Hotel to join the others for breakfast.

Jamling Tenzing was already waiting for us. We were surprised to see him. While his now-famous name appeared on our climbing permit and justified our formal expedition title, "the Indian-Canadian-American Siniolchu Expedition," he had decided to accompany a video crew from California shooting a documentary on Sherpas instead of joining us. A snow storm along the southern reaches of Kangchenjunga in the Dzongri area had interrupted this assignment, so now we had a chance to hash out last minute details with our absentee organizer.

During a prolonged meeting with him that morning, Jamling apologized for the fiasco in Delhi. "You guys were the first expedition to be processed under a new arrangement between the IMF and the Sikkim government," said the 35-year-old Sherpa. "The Sikkimese want more control over any expeditions coming into their jurisdiction. But they still don't know what they're doing. This will be the last time I organize an expedition in Sikkim."

"Sounds like we've got the same motto, Jamling," laughed Paul. "Never Again!"

Like many Sherpas, Jamling Tenzing comfortably straddles two cultures. He grew up in Darjeeling but received further education in the West at Wisconsin's Northland College. An American fleece jacket with an Everest IMAX badge sewn on its breast spoke of the man's worldliness. But prayer beads hanging from his neck suggested a traditional devotion to a Buddhist way of life.

Jamling, however, appeared burdened by his commitments to the bigger world, or perhaps by his role as the son of the famous Tenzing Norgay. When Jamling, the aspiring mountaineer, topped Everest on May 23, 1996 alongside Catalan climber Araceli Segarra, he followed his father's footsteps – in fact, he became the ninth member of his family to climb Everest. But his role as one of the principal characters in the Everest IMAX film now garnered some jealousy in local circles. One trekking

OVERLEAF. *Kangchenjunga is the protective deity of Sikkim. The massive mountain straddles the border of Nepal and the Indian state of Sikkim, and at 8595 meters is the third highest peak in the world.*

guide even called him "the Brad Pitt of the Himalaya," in reference to the Hollywood golden boy's recent role in the feature *Seven Years in Tibet.*

That afternoon Jamling invited us to a sumptuous lunch of Indian curries at his home. The video crew was also there, including a hip young sound technician with Darth Vader tattoos all over his legs. Throughout the meal he kept saying, "Oh, cool," as he downed one shot glass of Sikkim Bagpiper whiskey after another.

We sat on wide wooden benches cushioned by well-used carpets. More carpets padded the floor in traditional Sherpa fashion. As I looked about I realized that Jamling's house was really a museum of his father's exploits.

Tenzing died an international hero in 1986 at the age of 72. His climbing ability largely went unrecognized until his seventh expedition to Everest – the 1953 ascent with Edmund Hillary. That fame brought many rewards and responsibilities. As the first Field Director of the Himalayan Mountaineering Institute (founded in 1954 by India's Prime Minister Nehru), Tenzing popularized the sport of climbing throughout India. More importantly, he acted as an ambassador for the Sherpas, paving the way for their recognition as a unique people as well as high altitude specialists.

After lunch Jamling led us up a flight of creaky wooden stairs to a formal display of memorabilia behind locked glass cabinets. Personal treasures included curios collected during his father's guiding trip a half-century ago into Tibet with adventurous Italian scholar Giuseppe Tucci; one of the original oxygen bottles used on Everest in 1953; a photo of Tenzing mugging with New York Yankees slugger Mickey Mantle; and a stuffed toy penguin from a scientific research station in Antarctica. Even the baby shoe of Jamling's daughter found a place of honor. On a third floor, we entered the sanctity of an ornate prayer room where photos of Jamling's parents and His Holiness the Dalai Lama graced the altar. Numerous Buddhist scroll paintings framed in silk, called *thangkas*, covered the wall. Phuntsok Sanpo, the octogenarian Tibetan artist who painted them, lived next door.

The Sherpas are not native to Darjeeling. They migrated from eastern Tibet to the Khumbu region of Nepal several centuries ago. (In Tibetan, *sher* means east, and *pa,* people.) One hundred years ago the first Sherpas came to this British outpost from their homes around Everest to trade. Many stayed to earn good wages as rickshaw-wallahs and coolies. Pretty soon their strong work ethic brought them to the attention of expeditions heading off into the unexplored Himalaya.

The Norwegians first publicized the use of Sherpas as reliable porters in 1907. But it was Alexander Kellas, a Scottish doctor, who later championed their cause among international climbers and adventurers. Dr. Kellas made frequent forays into the Sikkim Himalaya between 1907 and 1921 to climb and trek, but with little fanfare. Partly due to his encyclopedic knowledge of the area, and his medical skills, Kellas was chosen to accompany the 1921 Everest Reconnaissance Expedition. Unfortunately, he picked up a case of dysentery. Weak and ailing he joined the team in Darjeeling only to die of complications a few weeks later at Khamba Dzong just inside Tibet. The team continued on with their Sherpas, hired at Kellas's urging, and, thereby, started a tradition.

IMAX's recent Everest film and Jon Krakauer's sensational best-seller, *Into Thin Air*, have now made these hardy people global icons. They are to Nepal what Everest is to the mountain world. Westerners who have trekked in these high mountains, such as the famous American author Peter Matthiessen, uniformly praise their good nature:

> The sherpas are alert for ways in which to be of use, yet are never insistent, far less servile; since they are paid to perform a service, why not do it as well as possible?… Yet their dignity is unassailable, for the service is rendered for its own sake – it is the task, not the employer, that is served. As Buddhists, they know that the doing matters more than the attainment or reward, that to serve in this selfless way is to be free. Because of their belief in karma – the principle of cause and effect that permeates Buddhism and Hinduism (and Christianity, for that matter; *as ye sow, so shall ye reap*) – they are tolerant and unjudgemental, knowing that bad acts will receive their due without the intervention of the victim.

On our trip we employed five Sherpas, including Jamling's uncle, 47-year-old Nima Norbu. For the trek to Mount Siniolchu, Nima served as our *sirdar*, a sort of camp foreman and manager. Nima, a resident of Darjeeling, came originally from Thame in the Khumbu region of Nepal. "But now I go back as a Sherpa tourist," he said with an infectious giggle.

The Sherpas were not the only Nepalis drawn to Darjeeling over the years. The British encouraged other hill tribes to come and work in the fields. During the mid 1880s, Darjeeling became a thriving hill resort for military and government officials of the British Raj. Colonials came here to drink gin and tonics and to take a break from the stifling heat and pestilence of the plains.

The British built an enduring legacy: Victorian bungalows with well-tended gardens, boarding schools and colleges (to educate Indians for the civil service), Christian churches and, most visible of all, sprawling tea plantations. As soon as the colonizers recognized the suitability of the soil and climate for tea cultivation, they smuggled in tea seeds from China. Entrepreneurs then cut down the local forest and replaced it with the lucrative bush. Seventy-eight tea "gardens" now employ more than 40,000 people in the lands around Darjeeling.

The promise of a better life still brings Nepalis to the region in great numbers. While walking along Tenzing Norgay Road, one of Darjeeling's winding streets, I even had the overpowering sensation of being in Nepal. I heard merchants speak in Nepali, and I saw short, squat Rai and Limbu men wearing their traditional garb: tight-legged, baggy-seated pants and double-breasted shirts tied at the side. Nepal's distinct *topi,* a brightly-colored, tassel-less version of a Shriner's hat, covered their heads. The women also dressed in typical Nepali fashion in long wrap-around skirts. Heavy gold nose rings decorated their walnut brown faces.

Back at our hotel we sipped some of Darjeeling's famous brew in a tiny dining room. There Jamling, who spends most of his time in Kathmandu these days, confessed that the state of his hometown now saddened him. "Darjeeling is no longer the same," he said. "In a place where it rains half of the year, there is a water shortage. There are constant power outages, and rampant corruption. It's not a pleasant place to live anymore."

Darjeeling's decline began when the Raj pulled out of India and West Bengal assumed power over the district's government. In the 1980s, Nepali-speaking immigrants, whose language is not recognized by the Indian Constitution, found their Bengali masters actively discriminating against them. All jobs in the civil service, for example, went to the Bengalis. Resentment bred riots, led by the Gurkha National Liberation Front that called for an independent hill state separate from West Bengal.

In 1988, a compromise led to the establishment of the Darjeeling Gurkha Hill Council. Once considered a model for other statehood movements in India, critics now accuse the agency of financial mismanagement and corruption. "Free Gurkha-land" graffiti and posters still remind the residents of Darjeeling of these enduring grievances.

Most of the colonial buildings today stand in various states of mold-streaked neglect. A springtime fog added to the gloom while we were there; people walked around huddled in shawls. The "Queen of the Hills" has sadly lost her charms.

Before leaving Darjeeling we sought out Dorjee Lhatoo, the Director of Field Training at the Himalayan Mountaineering Institute. In November of 1992 he had walked the full circuit around Kangchenjunga. After finding the handsome Tibetan at his institute, Dorjee invited us to his house down the hill. We followed in a taxi, as the Clint Eastwood-like Dorjee rode off on his motorbike.

Over tea and biscuits the 54-year-old quietly talked about his Kangchenjunga trek and his family's home in the idyllic Chumbi Valley just east of the Sikkimese border in Chinese-occupied Tibet. When Dorjee left Darjeeling on his 17-day trek, he not only followed Freshfield's footsteps but those of Frank Smythe.

In 1930 the British adventurer was part of an international team intent on the first ascent of Kangchenjunga via its northwest side in Nepal. When that attempt failed the expedition decided to take the long way back to Darjeeling. Instead of

St. Andrew's school, Darjeeling, in 1998

returning by way of Dzongri in southeastern Sikkim, Smythe and his party crossed Jonsong La to the north – the same high pass that Freshfield had navigated while going in the opposite direction.

Dorjee's team, made up mostly of Sherpas, traveled less conspicuously than his predecessors. Even so his group ran into problems along the border. The ever-vigilant Indo-Tibetan Border Police welcomed them in northern Sikkim with raised rifles. Nor was this the first time that Dorjee had come up against gun-wielding soldiers in the mountains. In 1970 Chinese troops opened fire on the mountaineer while he was climbing Chomolhari on the Bhutan border. We made a mental note to avoid such perils, and bid Dorjee farewell.

We left Darjeeling in a thick morning fog. Eight North Americans plus five Sherpas jammed into a small bus piled high with gear. I wore the *khata* scarf that Jamling had given each of us in farewell. According to Sherpa and Tibetan custom it is presented at meetings and leave-takings as a token of respect and good intentions. I hoped to find a high place somewhere near Kangchenjunga to leave the scarf as my humble offering.

St. Andrew's school, Darjeeling, in 1899. PHOTO: VITTORIO SELLA

Within an hour we arrived at the valley-bottom check-post at Rangpo. A brightly painted portal spanned the road and announced that we were entering Sikkim. Officials studiously examined and stamped our passports and permits, even though we were only passing from one Indian state into another.

Leah's unofficial status in our group raised more than a few eyebrows, but Nima, our attentive sirdar, did some fast talking. A friendly official entered our names into a big ledger and casually mentioned he was a collector of foreign coins. Eager to deflect any concern about our group, I found a lingering Canadian quarter in my wallet. "Very nice. Thank you, and what is this animal?" he said, turning the coin over. "It's a caribou, kind of like the serow stags that used to live in Sikkim," I said. With that, we officially entered the mythical Shangri-La.

For a while our bus followed the hot Tista Valley. Its river ran thick and brown with spring rain and glacial melt from the flanks of Kangchenjunga. We saw few villages. Towering *sal* hardwood trees dappled the road in welcome shade. Sikkim, which receives more than 3,000 millimeters of rain a year, is one of the wettest regions in all the Himalaya. This moisture makes the tiny state something of a naturalist's Eden.

Sir Joseph Hooker, the British botanist and naturalist, found an incredible diversity of plants and flowers in Sikkim. With plucky perseverance he tramped through its deep jungles and high mountains in 1848 and 1849: "Leeches were everywhere. They got into my hair, hung onto my eyelids, and crawled up my legs and my back." He made detailed descriptions of more than 2,900 species of Sikkim's plants, including 600 varieties of orchids and 30 kinds of rhododendrons. After the publication of his *Himalayan Journals* in 1854, the beauty of the country he described drew more and more curious Europeans. It was Hooker's simple map with its blank space in Kangchenjunga's northern perimeter that later encouraged Douglas Freshfield to "supply the missing links in the tour of Kangchenjunga."

Six hours after leaving Darjeeling, we ascended Sikkim's National Highway 31A to the state's hilltop capital. Our vehicle strained against gravity and traffic. A snarl of trucks, jeeps and mini-vans used as taxis jammed the steep, narrow road in an Indian version of road rage. Car horns blared like angry elephants ready to charge. Now nothing was moving in this city of 50,000 people.

"Gridlock in Gangtok," grumbled Pat, slamming the window shut as black, choking clouds of diesel exhaust gushed over our bus. I half-imagined a Buddhist-style genie, robes flowing and cymbals clanging, magically appearing out of the smoke to greet us. We had arrived, after all, in what tourist brochures call "The Land of Mystic Splendour" where enigmatic clouds swirl over idyllic monasteries deep in the lush mountains. Stuck in a traffic jam I realized that I would have to look beyond the concrete and noise to find any magic.

In Gangtok, bustling streets and new buildings collaborated to obliterate the landscape's charms. In this conspiracy Gangtok's urban sprawl has much global company. Quaint mountain towns all around the world, including Aspen, Zermatt and even our own Canmore, have fallen prey to rampant industrialized tourism. Nor is this a new story. One hundred years ago Freshfield wrote about the despoliation of the Alps with open disgust:

> Encircle a mountain with monster hotels; defile its valleys with the coal-smoke of engines that drag a perpetual merry-go-round of crowded cars; sprinkle its skyline with huts or barracks, capable at a pinch of holding a hundred guests; bind its crags in chains, and encourage suicide by marking out on them red tracks for guideless tourists, and it loses its primitive charm.

That's how we now felt about Gangtok. Four-to-five-storied buildings crammed a slope so precipitous that rooftops touched entranceways. Dozens more concrete structures grew from the mounds of sand and gravel that lay haphazardly in an obstacle course on the already crowded streets. Complicated webs of electrical wires spanned the sky. At ground level, unburied pipes the size of garden hoses branched off in logarithmic patterns as households and businesses alike competed for precious water. In the midst of so much hustle and bustle the only soothing sight was prayer flags, the omnipresent icons of Buddhist country. Attached to tall bamboo poles, the long, mostly white banners swayed gently in the breeze from rooftops and gardens like strands of seaweed bending in the ocean current. Their purpose was simple: to send prayers off to the heavens for the good of all sentient beings. They spoke of inner calmness amidst outer chaos.

Gangtok was not always such a noisome place. Just 50 years ago Giuseppe Tucci passed through the city. To the dedicated Tibetologist, Gangtok appeared as "a delightful little town, strewn like a wreath around the royal palace and the temple, with broad, park-like alleys, spic and span like a summer resort.... If the roads were repaired and the ban on the free entry of foreigners lifted, Sikkim would become one of the best mountain resorts of the whole of India." These days the central Indian government has surrendered Gangtok to raw commercialism. It needs to keep tourist dollars flowing to compensate for huge losses caused by the ongoing civil war in the once-idyllic tourist mecca of Kashmir.

We finally found tranquillity at the Mintokling Hotel. Graced with a beautiful flower garden, it sat high on the ridge just below the Royal Palace, beyond the fray of the mushrooming city. The building was renovated recently; its doors and windows had been painted with bright traditional designs of lotus flowers and dragons.

In the garden we sipped lukewarm, locally brewed Dansberg beers and admired the snowy brow of Kangchenjunga. To the east, Siniolchu cut the sky like a silver sword. The mountains looked disarmingly close.

"Well, folks," ventured Ace. "I believe we have an expedition on our hands." We clinked our glasses in a rallying toast and downed our beers.

Next morning while the others still slept, Pat and I headed out for a walk to stretch our legs. Early mornings are always pleasant wherever you are in the Himalaya. We strolled along the broad, ridge-top promenade lined with tall eucalyptus trees. A crescendo of car horns oddly blended in with the dissonant rumble of monks' horns in a morning *puja,* a ceremony of recitation and worship.

We passed the gates of the Royal Palace, where Prince Wanchuk, the last in the line of a 300-year-old monarchy, lives. Deprived of his kingdom he now meditates and prays in hermit-like seclusion. The Indian government is so wary of this vestige of the old Sikkim that the gates remain closed except for New Year's celebrations.

Sikkim's loss of independence still irks many of its people. They feel that the Indian government deceived pro-democracy forces when it invaded in 1975 on the pretense of quelling riots. Later that day we met a businessman who was closely related to the royal family. He knew much about the political manipulation that had taken place.

"The Sikkimese people were tricked," he explained, sadly shaking his head. "During the referendum we thought we were being asked whether we wanted more democracy. Of course we wanted this. But we didn't want the Indian army coming

OVERLEAF. *Sikkim's capital city, Gangtok, sprawls across the*
foothills high above the Ranipul River.

25

in. The riots that took place here were part of India's ploy. They brought in people from Darjeeling to participate." Official versions of events simply note that Sikkim happily joined India in 1975.

It was now too late for this tiny Buddhist realm to reverse the course of history. (At 110 kilometers deep by 65 kilometers long, Sikkim is no bigger than New Delhi and its outlying suburbs.) India, which coveted Sikkim's strategic low mountain passes for years, basically grabbed them for security reasons. Chinese aggression has always been one of India's biggest worries, and Sikkim made a good defensive cushion.

The Chinese threat is very real. Most Indians still remember China's attacks near their eastern Burmese border and in the western region of Ladakh in 1962. At the time the ill-equipped Indian army could do little to prevent the invasions. Nor were they the last of China's incursions. In 1967 the Chinese once again fought Indian troops at Natu La, just 54 kilometers from Gangtok.

A fellow Mintokling lodger, a middle-aged doctor visiting from Calcutta with her family, clearly recalled the latest invasion. "I was a teenaged girl then. We thought the Chinese were going to invade us. We had city-wide blackouts, and air raid practices. India had no weapons at the time, and we felt so vulnerable."

During our morning walk in Gangtok the intrigues of war seemed part of another time and place. We found a modest monastery sitting on the prow of a wooded ridge just below the 60-meter-high TV tower. Enchey Gompa had been built in 1909 on the site of the hermitage of the Tantric master Lama Druptob Karpo. According to legend he arrived at the spot by flying across Sikkim. I pictured a figure from a Chagall painting freewheeling through the sky.

For the next two days we spent most of our time getting ready for the expedition. That first morning Paul, crippled by a queasy "Delhi Belly," bravely headed off to finalize the Inner Line permit that would allow us to proceed beyond the city. "What would a day in India be without a visit to a government office?" he said in parting. Luckily he had not lost his sense of humor.

The rest of us passed the morning with a visit to the State Bank of India to exchange money. Normally this is not a daunting task. But in Gangtok, converting a lump of coal into a gold ingot might be easier. The sign at the bank's doorway greatly misled us: "Welcome to our fully computerized branch." There were computers; I even saw them. But they served some other mysterious purpose than that of facilitating transactions.

I approached a bank employee who sat behind a wide desk in the crowded room. A small dog lay tucked at her feet. When I pushed a handful of US$20 bills in front of her, she looked quite dismayed. "Don't you have any larger bills?" she asked.

I shook my head, and she sighed as she began to painstakingly write down the serial numbers from each of the bills first in one ledger and then in a second one. That completed, she passed the money and my passport across to the next desk to her superior, who then copied it all over again into a third ledger. Afterwards, I was given a coin-like chit with a number on it and told to go downstairs to wicket number three. There I waited in a crowded passageway until someone in a caged enclosure finally grabbed my chit. The clerk counted out rupee notes from a huge wad stapled together. Then he ripped off the ragged-eared bills and passed them to me.

Paul dragged himself back to the hotel at mid-day with more bureaucratic war stories. He had languished for three and a half hours in the office of Tsegyal Tashi, Deputy Secretary of the Sikkim Home Department.

"Remember those 10 passport photos we had to send in with the permit application?" asked Paul. "Well, believe it or not, we still need one more for the Inner Line permit." Paul's sarcasm was getting edgy. "Then they asked for all the papers from the Sikkim Home Office in Delhi. But guess what? The Dragon Lady kept them! So Mr. Tashi, nice guy by the way, called and got them to fax the papers. But the fax was too faint to read. He called back and then guess what he did?" Paul's voice was nearly hysterical by this point. "The entire document was dictated over the phone, which he in turn relayed to a lackey who typed it out! Can you believe it?" This had taken over an hour. "Never again!" cried Paul. He then slumped into his chair like a rag doll with half of its stuffing removed. We pushed a glass of beer into his hand.

Even our lead Sherpa, Nima, a man blessed with wells of Buddhist patience and much climbing experience, shook his head at our untoward dealings with the government. "Too much harassment," he said. We laughed. Nima's English was sometimes incomprehensible because of his accent and grammar, but his sophisticated word described our situation perfectly.

Paul had also learned a useful bit of information: 50 centimeters of snow had fallen near Lachen, our trail head to Kangchenjunga. This news troubled us. No matter how prepared and good a climbing team is, the weather inevitably decides an expedition's success or failure.

"This winter was very strange," added Nima. "Very dry until late March. Then clouds came, and there was much snow." A month before our arrival a gargantuan avalanche had wiped out 19 Indian soldiers at Thangu, an army base just north of Lachen. In concert with our spirits, the day clouded over and peals of thunder rolled across the valley.

Ugen, our ever-faithful liaison officer, duly arrived with the good news that all money transactions with the Sikkim Home Office had gone smoothly. Now it was time to get him outfitted for the high mountains. At the Lal Bazaar, I wandered amidst haggling locals and patient vendors hawking their wares: mounds of yellow turmeric and red chili powders, and cardamom (Sikkim's main cash crop); strings of dried cheese called *churpi* and heaps of smelly dried fish.

Nima and Pasang came along to help with the bargaining. We had already provided Nima with expedition clothing, as per IMF rules. But most of it never got used. Many Sherpas simply store the gear, using their old clothes instead, and then sell it at the end of the expedition to supplement their take-home pay. We now picked out an insulated jacket and pair of hiking boots for Ugen. Due to a trucker's strike there was no kerosene available for our stoves. But the merchants assured us that we would be able to buy some from the army in Lachen. "Under the table," whispered Nima. Everyone in our group bought umbrellas. I purchased a string of brightly colored prayer flags to hang at base camp.

The next day, after breakfast we piled our duffel bags outside the hotel. We were finally ready to leave – almost. Then Paul went dashing off to fetch a final piece of paper with Leah's name added to it. We passed the time watching TV. Thanks to satellites, even this remote outpost was bombarded by drivel being broadcast from the world we had come so far to leave behind.

After Paul returned with the document, Nima announced our plans. The climbing gear, food and the Sherpas would go in a truck. The eight of us plus himself would cram into one jeep for the 155-kilometer journey to Lachen. We protested loudly. There was no way all of us could sanely fit into that jeep. After much discussion, the hotel manager agreed to rent us its car for part of the way. At Mangan, he instructed us, we could find another four-wheel-drive and send the Mintokling's car back.

The single-lane, blacktopped road was in surprisingly good condition, considering the precipitous terrain it traveled. Occasionally a landslide had ripped out a culvert or parts of the road. Our vehicle then had to crawl through stream beds or over rocky debris. After crossing one wide creek that plummeted into a waterfall just below the road, I watched with dismay as our jeep driver pumped the now useless brake pedal with his bare foot in an effort to get rid of the water, all the while maneuvering around sinuous blind corners. Fortunately it was not raining. The monsoon season that would soon bring heavy rain usually creates havoc, as it had the previous June, when more than 50 people died in severe landslides around Gangtok. The mangled steel skeleton of a bridge that we passed served as a grim reminder of nature's capriciousness.

Like all roads this one had spelled the end of wilderness in the region. In Freshfield's time the land was truly a remarkable Eden, "something fantastic and fabulous." His party rode for five days on horseback from Gangtok to Lachen through a steamy, luxuriant tangle of bamboo, magnolia and hydrangea. As the Europeans climbed higher, the jungle gave way to cool forests of rhododendron, pine and larch.

But since the appearance of the road the jungle and the forest has largely disappeared near Gangtok where land-hungry peasants have cut down the trees to make room for terraces. Because of their precarious hold on the near-vertical slopes, the newcomers live poorly. But compared to Nepal, where agriculture has supplanted the natural forest cover of most valleys from top to bottom, Sikkim still has much greenery left.

At Chungthang the Lachung and the Lachen tributaries join to form Sikkim's main river, the Tista. While it may have once been an idyllic spot, inspiring a name that means "the Meadows of Marriage (of two rivers)" the settlement now boasted a large army camp. A soldier, bundled in an insulated jacket and wool cap in preparation for the mountain night, squeezed into the front seat of our jeep to escort us the rest of the way to Lachen. Even with the military aboard, we still had to wave our permits in the face of sleepy-eyed guards as we passed through an extensive munitions camp filled with No Smoking signs.

As we rumbled up the narrow confines of the Lachen Valley in the late afternoon, a vibrant double rainbow spanned the forested ridges. It seemed to be more auspicious sign than all the soldiers. By darkness, we were in Lachen.

Chapter 2

UP THE ZEMU

IN THE DARK OF NIGHT A LONE FIGURE ACCOSTED US JUST AS WE were about to stash our gear in the government compound at Lachen. "I am Lalit, the school teacher. I will be your guide," he said authoritatively. "I can tell you all about Sikkim."

His strangely troubled eyes reflected the dim light of our kerosene lantern like those of a caged leopard.

"Come back tomorrow," we urged him. Exhausted from the day's long journey from Gangtok, we retreated to the Guru Dongmar Lodge, the village's only guest house.

The morning found this remote village waking with traditional Buddhist ritual. From hanging braziers delicate curls of juniper smoke purified the brisk mountain air. An old man sat on his front porch, spinning his prayer wheel and muttering mantras as the sun crept into the valley. Like most of the villagers he was a Bhutia – of Tibetan stock – and looked as hardy as the mountains he lived in. Freshfield astutely observed that the average Tibetan seemed as though "he were a survival from an ice age." This elder fit the description perfectly. Wind and cold had etched deep crevasses on his face. Through narrow slits his eyes turned towards us. I greeted him with the Tibetan "*Tashi Delek!*" He barely nodded in response, intent on spiritual matters.

Lhatsun Lepcha, dressed in traditional garb for a ceremony, is a young Lepcha man whose ancestors were the original forest inhabitants of Sikkim. His people now make up less than one-fifth of the population.

As we ventured beyond our guest house, we carefully stepped over the steaming patties of cow dung dotting the main street. And then we heard a familiar voice.

"Good morning, my friends!"

The vigilant Lalit bounded into view. "How are you? You sleep OK?" he asked. Today, he was in a cheerful mood and chattered on like a hyperactive Himalayan marmot.

"Please, now listen. Here is a joke. Why don't Indians make good soccer players?" he asked, pausing for effect. "Because every time they get into a corner, they open up a shop."

We laughed appreciatively. Having caught our attention Lalit began to describe his athletic achievements. He said he had been a table tennis champion and a star soccer player. But when he started talking about cricket, Paul lost his diplomacy. "Cricket? That's a bug!" The tone of his voice as much as his comment prompted our hapless guide to walk away. We promised to meet him later and then toured the village on our own.

The villagers of Lachen in northern Sikkim are Bhutias — of Tibetan stock — and have strong religious and cultural ties with their neighbors across the border.

Like most of Sikkim's villages, Lachen, at an altitude of 2730 meters, is squeezed on a claustrophobic cleft between deeply forested mountains. Because the location leaves little room for cultivation, villagers plant potato fields and herd their yaks and goats at Thangu, 28 kilometers up the road where the valley opens up.

Thanks to commerce brought by the Indian army and the road it maintains, Lachen's main street has a few small shops and even a video parlor. Lucrative military contracts have enabled a few villagers to build large concrete houses and own fashionable Mahindra jeeps. Two more guest houses were under construction in anticipation of moneyed visitors. Tourism, the panacea for yanking poor farmers out of their subsistence existence, was bulldozing its way up another Himalayan valley.

But off the main thoroughfare, old village ways pleasingly persisted. Handsome two-storied wooden houses, all adorned with tall prayer flag poles, stood in close quarters. Only the smallest of gardens and a few apple trees, now in full bloom, could fit in between. Space, after all, is a precious commodity in a state where just about everyone lives on a vertical hillside.

Below the village the silty waters of the Lachen River churned with the melted snows coming from the northeast slopes of Kangchenjunga, some 50 kilometers away. From its source near the Tibetan border the river descends 3,000 meters in a space of less than 80 kilometers to Chungthang. Not surprisingly, hydroelectric engineers have channeled Sikkim's abundant water into installations that electrify 95 percent of the state's villages. But at the moment, Lachen remained in darkness. Eight months ago a landslide destroyed its mini-hydro plant. Nobody knew when the electricity would be restored.

On our Lachen walkabout we met Sonam Bhutia, the amicable administrator of the government arts and handicrafts program. Inside the large, two-storied cement building, students aged 14 and older learned how to card and spin wool, and weave Tibetan carpets. The boys carved wooden wall hangings of dragons or one of Buddhism's eight auspicious symbols such as the conch shell (representing the call to rise from ignorance and follow noble deeds) and the lotus flower (symbol of purity).

This program impressed me. India is not known for upholding the rights of its children. More than 60 million youth now work in textile factories, some chained to machines. Pay amounts to little more than two inadequate meals a day. In contrast, the teenagers at Lachen's school received 300 to 350 rupees a month (US$8–9). And the skills they learned at the handicrafts program allowed them to earn extra income during the winter, when they didn't have to work in the fields. All smiles, our group left the building with newly purchased carpets and mats under our arms.

Sonam also agreed to show us Lachen's *gompa* a short distance above the village. Sikkim is home to more than a hundred Buddhist monasteries. The administrator heaved his two-year-old son, Karma, onto his back and led the way up the steep trail in his flip-flops.

Gompa means "solitary place," and isolation from the world has always been a great desideratum for Buddhist monks. Peace and quiet help them avoid mundane distractions. This monastery, although not terribly isolated from the town, occupied an idyllic clearing surrounded by trees. Originally founded in 1806, it had been ebuilt recently with mortar and cement. Yellow paint brightened the wood around the pagoda-style roof and windows. Vibrant murals of the celestial kings, guardians of the world's four quarters, boldly protected the entrance. These demonic-looking figures have the power to ward off evil from these places where goodness is taught.

"You must first walk around the gompa three times for good luck," Sonam instructed. And we did. As we were about to enter, Lalit caught up with us, breathless and angry.

"Where were you? I was waiting for you in my room, but you didn't come," he said in a reproachful voice.

"We're sorry. We couldn't find you," said Ali, always the tactful mediator.

Kina Lachenpa, the caretaker monk, unlocked the door for us. Leaving our shoes at the entrance, we stepped into the large, cool prayer hall illuminated by scant window light. Sonam, Nima and Lalit prostrated three times.

I watched Lalit perform his religious observances. With palms pressed together, he first lifted them above his head and then touched them to his forehead, mouth and heart in a fluid movement. This signified the unity of mind, speech and body. He knelt and bent his forehead to the ground in a final act of humility.

Earlier that morning Lalit had proudly shown me a plastic ring bearing an image of Sai Baba, a popular guru with an ashram near Bangalore in the state of Karnataka. ("It cost only 3 rupees, but it is very special," explained Lalit.) I recognized Sai Baba's face from posters on sale in Gangtok's Lal Bazaar. The orange-robed spiritual master with a serene smile and frizzy Afro hairdo apparently commands a large following among Indians and Westerners.

"I also believe in Christianity," Lalit added. The teacher's eclectic approach to spirituality is very common in the Himalaya. Mountain people borrow freely from a pantheon of deities and demons whenever need arises. Lalit was just playing it safe by covering all bases.

The monastery's 80 monks had retreated to Gangtok, leaving only Kina Lachenpa to tend to the daily rituals. The gentle-mannered man replenished the butter lamps; their tiny flames help vanquish the darkness of ignorance. He refreshed the seven small bowls of water that lined the altar. They are the simplest of offerings – a gift of one's pure nature in the eyes of the Buddha. The elaborate wall murals, exquisitely painted by Bhutanese craftsmen, seemed to glow in the gompa's dimness. Some deities writhed in demonic wrathfulness, exhorting believers to abandon all vices and weaknesses. Others, smiling with love and compassion, depicted the peaceful path to Buddhahood.

As we walked around the gompa's main room, Sonam explained the images. To Tibetan Buddhists whose word for painter means "writer of gods," art is not regarded as an end in itself but as a vehicle to help realize a higher spiritual path. The monks who live in Sikkim's many gompas do not paint for themselves but for the merit of all beings, be they maggots or men. Sonam made it clear to us that Buddhism is both a way of believing and a way of being in Sikkim.

On the second floor, we entered another dark room that housed the *Kanjur,* the sacred scriptures of Tibetan Buddhism. Wrapped in cloth between two pieces of wood, the rectangular, unbound volumes were stored in cubbyholes along the wall. Next to the Kanjur sat a very special icon in a glass case on the altar. The caretaker monk unlocked it and proudly held out a granite slab bearing a perfect footprint.

"It is of Guru Rinpoche," remarked Sonam, referring to the Indian sage who introduced Buddhism to Tibet in the 8th century. Guru Rinpoche, a most prolific walker, remarkably left evidence of his travels throughout the countryside. Relics of his passage dot the Himalayan countryside as distinctly as medicine wheels on the Canadian Plains. On a trek through western Nepal in the 1950s the British scholar David Snellgrove bumped into one Guru Rinpoche shrine after another: "One is led to reflect once more on the ubiquity of this wonder-working master of religion, who is supposed to have passed along almost every route that connects Tibet with India."

Pat and I had seen signs of Guru Rinpoche's wanderings elsewhere in the Himalaya. In 1997, we walked the ancient pilgrim's trail around Mount Bönri. This mountain in the Kongpo region of southeastern Tibet is sacred to followers of Bön, an animist precursor to Buddhism. In a grove of junipers we found prayer flags surrounding a big boulder with two vague indentations. One was the footprint of Guru Rinpoche and the other of Kuchok Ripa Drukse, the hermit who established the route in the 14th century. Other trail-side attractions included symbolic thrones, drums, hand prints and even a body print of the "Precious Guru". We also found small notched branches representing ladders, called *Zhingkham Dzekke,* "the ladders to Paradise." And in a nearby place called *Dhikpa Dhotak,* the "sin-stone tying place," transgressors hung stones with red strings on the branches of a tree. The entire trail represented a fantastical netherworld where the forces of good and evil eternally fought each other.

A monk at Lachen monastery proudly displays a sacred relic: the footprint left in stone by Guru Rinpoche, the sage who introduced Buddhism into Tibet in the 8th century.

Guru Rinpoche's footprint at Lachen looked entirely genuine. The rock distinctly showed the impression of a whole foot, toes and all, something similar to what you might find embedded in concrete on Hollywood's Boulevard of Stars. Before putting the granite slab away, the monk touched the sacred relic to the little boy's forehead as a blessing. On the spur of the moment I bobbed my head down to it as well.

"It can't hurt," I said. "We need all the luck we can get." The others followed suit and we left the monastery, blessed and satiated.

Besides luck, we needed 40 porters. A government decree specified that we had to deal with a village contractor who, in turn, received a commission for wrangling porters. He took 50 percent of the wages, leaving the porters with 85 rupees per day (US$2.20). The rules also stated that every six porters must have a seventh along to carry their food. But in reality the seventh never showed and everyone carried their own provisions. More money for the contractor, I thought.

"What kind of porter mafia is this anyway?" asked RJ who, like Paul, questioned the rule-bound world of the Himalaya. Although baffled by the system at first, we later learned that a good portion of the contractor's 50 percent actually went to a pension plan and village fund to help injured or sick porters.

On short notice the local contractor could only round up 20 porters. Most of the men were at Thangu planting the potato fields. In the end the porters agreed to carry double loads with our essentials, and the contractor promised to send along another dozen men to base camp with the rest of our supplies as soon as possible.

At the government compound we rearranged our gear and food for the trek to Siniolchu. Lacking a hand-held scale, we used a 25 kilogram bag of rice as a counterweight for measuring loads for our porters. A gaggle of ragtag kids pressed up against the high, barbed-wire fence around the enclosure to watch this curious circus of an expedition.

Their curiosity gave us the impression that foreigners rarely came here. Yet nearly a hundred years ago Sikkim was an important gateway to Tibet as well as a popular destination for travelers.

The British certainly made trekking a civilized pastime. During the last century they built not only trails up these valleys but also government rest houses, called *dak* bungalows. Situated at intervals of one-day marches, these wayside lodges dotted the route all the way from Darjeeling to Thangu. To this day Lachen's run-down dak bungalow still houses travelers, mostly government and army officials.

All of these bungalows kept a visitor's registry that recorded the comings and goings of the famous and not so famous. Lachen's book, stolen several years ago, probably contained some very illustrious names and stories. Just about any climber involved in the early attempts on Everest, Kangchenjunga or a host of lesser peaks passed through Lachen.

Mountaineers were not the only ones interested in Sikkim. In the 19th century both the British and Russian governments played a lively version of the Cold War throughout central Asia, known to historians as the "Great Game." The two powers mistrusted each other's political interests so fiercely that Tibet, the aloof middleman, was alternately courted and threatened by both sides.

To gather intelligence and procure maps of the remote border passes the British sent out carefully trained Indian spies. Disguised as pilgrims and holy men, these "pundits" penetrated Tibet and surveyed its unmapped expanses in the most ingenious ways. They used Buddhist rosaries with 100 prayer beads instead of the requisite

Our trek to Mt. Siniolchu started from Lachen. Its Nyingma monastery overlooks the village.

108 to keep track of the paces they walked. And they carried handheld prayer wheels with false bottoms to hide intelligence notes and a compass.

Douglas Freshfield, our historical mentor, immediately recognized the value of the pundits. Before setting out for Kangchenjunga from Darjeeling, he hired a pundit named Rinsing Namgyal. Under the employ of the British Raj, Rinsing made the very first circuit around Kangchenjunga in 1884. Freshfield particularly relied on the native guide to get his party safely over Jonsong La at 6145 meters on the north side of the mountain. Thanks to Rinsing's knowledge and in spite of deep snow they safely made it across what Rinsing described as "the Jaws of Death."

Freshfield was not the only one to make good use of pundits. When Everest became the obsession of mountaineers in the early 1900s, Captain John Noel carefully studied the accounts of the pundit Sarat Chandra Das before heading out. In 1913 he set out from Darjeeling and stopped in Lachen to pick up porters and guides. Disguised as a "Mohammedan from India," Noel then tried a secret route behind Kangchenjunga to the gorge of the Arun that had been first explored by the pundit. Tibetan soldiers turned him back just 65 kilometers from Everest.

Noel, determined to see the mountain, returned in 1922 as the official photographer on the first British expedition to Everest. That team entered Tibet via Jelep La and finally rewarded Noel with an Everest vista. Two years later, the Everest addict again returned as a member of the infamous 1924 expedition, which made world headlines when George Mallory and Andrew Irvine disappeared close to the summit.

But of all the early travelers to Sikkim, Alexandra David-Neel was the most fascinating. With the support of a generous husband who was a railway executive in Tunisia, the French adventuress journeyed throughout the Himalaya and wrote twenty books about her experiences. To this day Orientalists recognize the tenacious traveler as a great scholar of Tibetan Buddhism.

She was also the first white woman to enter the holy city of Lhasa. Accompanied by Yongden, a young Sikkimese who became her life-long assistant and companion, David-Neel traveled to Tibet in 1914 and 1915. When she couldn't get near the forbidden Tibetan capital, she and Yongden tried another route. That circuitous journey took them to Beijing in 1917, after passing through Burma, Japan and Korea. From there they made their way to Kumbum in Mongolia, one of Buddhism's richest and most important monasteries. David-Neel stayed "in the lulling calm of the monastic citadel" for nearly three years. Her husband apparently did not mind her long absences.

Several years later, at the age of 55, David-Neel finally arrived in Lhasa disguised as a Tibetan beggar. She looked every inch the part, with hair dyed black by Chinese ink and skin darkened by a paste of cocoa and charcoal. Although greatly weakened by her hardships she managed to return to Europe to write about her adventures.

David-Neel also spent some time near Lachen exploring the Lhonak Valley on the north side of Kangchenjunga. In 1915 she sought out an anchorite who lived on a hilltop at 4000 meters near Thangu. She begged the holy man to let her over-winter in a cave retreat near his own rocky abode. He was reluctant at first, but she persuaded him of her integrity. The learned monk coached her in advanced meditation techniques and revealed insights into the practices of many famous mystics. At the end of a long winter of introspection, the Himalayan spring melted David-Neel out of her reverie.

She wrote lovingly of this prolonged stay in her book *Magic and Mystery In Tibet:*

> Nine hundred feet below my cave rhododendrons blossomed. I climbed barren mountain tops. Long tramps led me to desolate valleys studded with translucent lakes.… Solitude, solitude!… Mind and senses develop their sensibility in this contemplative life made up of continual observations and reflections. Does one become a visionary or, rather, is it not that one has been blind until then?

On April 28th, we strode out of Lachen, as intent and single-minded in our expedition as David-Neel had been in her ambition to reach Lhasa. A crowd of gawking children watched as we left. Sonam bid us farewell: "The gods will be with you. You have said your prayers."

At the last moment, Lalit intercepted us and handed me a photo he had taken of an orchid. "You are my friends," he said in parting. The sun shone brightly and we were full of hope as we passed a line of tall poles with flapping prayer flags at the edge of town. We were glad to be walking again.

The first six kilometers of our trek followed the one-lane road that led to Thangu. A convoy of army trucks rattled by, and when the last one stopped, we cordially greeted its occupant. Our IMF permit specifically warned us not to have any contact with military personnel. One soldier stuck his hand out the window and regaled us in Hindi. I reciprocated with a hand shake. But when he refused to let go and squeezed my hand in a covetous way, I smacked it hard against the door.

Around the next bend Kit and Ali had fared no better. "Those slimy soldiers in the army trucks kept leering at us as if they'd never seen women before," said Kit. While many of the soldiers had been genuinely friendly, several obviously could not resist the sight of foreign women striding up the road. While objective dangers are inevitable on any adventure in the Himalaya, this sort of harassment unfortunately is also part of the package.

As soon as we crossed the Zemu River, our trail left the road and veered west towards Siniolchu. Fed by the greatest of Kangchenjunga's glaciers this fast and deep river once served as the boundary between Sikkim and Tibet. Above us, spring melt water from alpine slopes cascaded down into a delicate waterfall. A carpet of white-blossomed strawberry plants lined the trail, promising a sweet feast later on.

"Welcome to the Republic of Zemu," Ace said. It was, indeed, a mountain kingdom of incomparable beauty. Steep granitic ridges shored up the gateway to the narrow Zemu Valley. Further up virgin old growth forests provided welcome shade.

"We should all set our watches to Zemu mountain time," joked Ali. But as on most expeditions the easiest thing, we decided, was to simply ignore them. Pat and I have never been in the habit of wearing a watch. On the trail, it stays tucked in a pack, serving only as a reference point when needed.

The twisted branches of rhododendrons made any pretense of deviating off the path impossible. I now appreciated why the early explorers had experienced such hardship coming up this valley. Freshfield even employed "Gurkha pioneers" to slash a trail through the botanical maze.

Although locals still graze their livestock up the lower Zemu Valley, they cannot do so in the higher alpine meadows. The upper reaches now fall within the boundaries of Kangchenjunga National Park, Sikkim's largest ecological reserve. Locals do, however, still poach the wild animals in the park. We found evidence of their work, including the discarded hide of a *bharal,* or blue sheep. Further up the valley at the Yabuk campsite, we discovered a snare made out of electrical wire along with the skin of a musk deer. It had been killed to feed the insatiable Asian market for traditional medicines.

Everywhere we walked along the Zemu the mountains demonstrated their innate power. At four different places landslides had torn open the earth, leaving loose debris. Now hut-sized boulders balanced above the trail. The next good rainfall would send them plummeting into the river. We scuttled across the unstable slopes, careful of our footing.

At the end of our first day in the Zemu the afternoon's clouds coagulated into mist and grayness. A spray of rain hit our entourage just as we arrived at Yedang at 3200 meters. Hurriedly, we pitched our tents. Some porters strung up a makeshift shelter with a plastic tarp in the trees while others huddled under a giant overhanging boulder.

The Lachen porters, a mix of old and young men, were a study in simplicity. Equipped with little more than a blanket, a fire-blackened cooking pot and some food, they could travel anywhere. We, on the other hand, came burdened with all our worldly props and vices, not to mention multiple changes of high-tech clothing. No wonder our duffel bags bulged. Ace took the prize for having the most pairs of footwear: sandals, runners, hiking boots, rock shoes (in case he wanted to go bouldering), plastic climbing boots and insulated booties for tent use on the mountain. Lao Tzu, the ancient Chinese poet, had a kernel of wisdom for us: "Have little and you will gain; Have much and you will be confused."

To our porters we must have looked like a strange and wealthy lot. Our brightly colored clothing made of miracle fabrics, some even spun from recycled pop bottles, stood in stark contrast to their minimalist non-waterproof cotton and wool garments. We wore hundred-dollar hiking boots; they wore cheap rubber ones. While most of our outer gear was waterproof, they warded off the rain by throwing lightweight plastic sheets over themselves. A few of the younger porters had gone modern. They owned imitation leather jackets and wore paisley printed scarves wrapped around their heads, pirate-style.

Our camping place stood at the confluence of the Lhonak and Zemu Rivers, where early explorers marveled at the opportunities for trekking and climbing. When British expeditions passed through Sikkim on their way home from Everest in 1933, 1936 and 1938, a few of the climbers, like Bill Tilman ("with some unexpected time on my hands"), made detours to the Lhonak Valley to test themselves on unclimbed peaks. But after World War II border politics restricted this part of Sikkim to Indian military personnel. Abandoned army bunkers in the Zemu served as a spooky reminder of their stay.

While the rain kept us tent bound Pat and I read an account of a two-man 1976 expedition to this region. Harish Kapadia and Zerksis Boga, two mountaineers from Bombay, were the first civilians allowed to visit the area in more than a decade. During their 240-kilometer trek they crossed over a series of four high passes including Tangchung La (5150 meters) and Lhonak La (5035 meters). I longed to take off and explore these places without permits or liaison officers.

The next morning brought more rain. "So Nima, where's the sun today?" asked Paul, looking at the sodden skies. "Oh, gone with the wind," he replied with his now familiar giggle. We worried about snow blocking our way higher up the valley. Knowing that we only had a short distance to cover to the next camp, we lingered over breakfast and waited for the downpour to stop.

Just beyond the camp, we faced a rickety, 10-meter-long bridge across the Lhonak River. It looked as though the weight of any foreigner might suddenly break the structure and send it into the frothy water below. We undid the waist belts of our packs and stepped across gingerly.

Our burdened porters, however, crossed the bridge nonchalantly. They carried their cargo on their backs, Himalayan-style, with a tump line slipped over their foreheads. Some used polyester webbing that was obviously cast-off from previous expeditions, while others relied on handmade ropes of strong yak hair to bind their loads.

Rubber boots now proved to be the footwear of choice. Nima, who wanted to keep his runners clean and dry across the soggy meadows, switched to flip-flops and rolled up his pant legs. The rest of us donned gaiters and slopped through the water and mud. But wherever a clearing provided access to light, clusters of mauve-colored primulas brightened up our path. Spring was pushing through a winter-toughened ground in spurts of green. Aromatic shoots of wild onions grew profusely on a sunsoaked riverbank.

The trail swung away from the riverbed to a steeply inclined meadow, and then plunged back down to the riverside near our next campsite at Jakthang. (Or "Yak Dung" as some in our party liked to mispronounce it.) We had gained only about 200 meters in elevation from Yedang, yet it was enough to put us at the edge of snow line. By one of nature's strange designs the rhododendrons drooping over the river bloomed with flowers the same hue as the off-colored snow. The others we had seen all sported shades of red, from a pale chartreuse to a rich choke-cherry.

Much to our surprise, we found a wooden hut raised up on stilts at the riverside camp. Its roof had caved in, and charcoal-inscribed graffiti, a legacy of previous Indian visitors, covered the walls. A sign implored users to keep things clean and not to shit near the river. But rusted tin cans and broken whiskey bottles lay scattered around old fire rings. On our return, Nima and Sangay, one of the Sherpas, gathered up loads of rubbish and buried it in the woods.

The dilapidated hut provided a niche for Pasang's kitchen and a shelter for some of the porters. They never needed much to make themselves at home. Pasang positioned a big tin of fruit on the floor to use as a stool and began to chop up vegetables and make chapatis. Jamling had introduced Pasang as "the best cook in Sikkim," and in these rustic circumstances, his culinary skills proved his reputation.

Pasang had catered to expeditions all over the Himalaya. He even worked on a Russian expedition that successfully completed a traverse of the main peaks of Kangchenjunga in 1989. After the climbers left base camp, Pasang's responsibilities were

Sikkim's forests of oak, maple, rhododendron, fir and juniper are some of the finest in the Himalaya, thanks to Sikkim's population of only 420,000 (low compared to neighboring Nepal, where 21 million strain natural resources).

46

minimal. The Sherpa put his hands to the side of his face, mimicking a sleeping posture. "I rest in base camp – 40 days – sleeping, sleeping!" he laughed.

One of the Lachen porters, clad in a pink wool hat and red, shin-high rubber boots, helped out with the chores and brought us tea the next morning. The British trekking tradition of bed tea at tent side was most welcome here, and our crew provided the finest breakfast service.

The sun rose and soon evaporated steam from our soggy tents. As we gathered around breakfast, I announced to everyone the real reason for the good weather. "It's our wedding anniversary today. Fourteen years of bliss and...." I looked at Pat to fill in the gap but knew I would not get a serious answer from him.

"Yeah, congratulations for putting up with me for so long," came the reply. I felt pretty lucky, nonetheless. It's not often that you can find a partner who becomes your companion in work and play. I headed up the Zemu with a light step and a smile.

At 15 degrees Celsius, the temperature was perfect for hiking. Avalanches, or what a Canadian friend calls "big gully washers," had ripped down one side of the valley and bulldozed their way almost a hundred meters up the other. Hiking atop this still hard surface was far preferable to plodding through the dense and tangled forest.

Several hours later, the trail swung unexpectedly up a dry, south-facing avalanche path for a long distance. Just as we began to have concerns that we were lost, a steep track appeared, cut up through a dense belt of thorny bushes. We climbed over the crest of the ridge and emerged from the claustrophobic clutter of the valley into the openness of the sub-alpine zone. A Daphne pheasant, flushed from its roost, chortled in protest.

At Yabuk, a pasture cut by a tiny brook, a two-story wooden structure welcomed us. The porters quickly moved into the rundown shack while our better-equipped Sherpas used a lean-to for their cooking. We pitched our tents on sparse grass that clung to an alluvial fan further up.

The gentle warmth of the sun and a vista of snowy peaks made the place all the more inviting. We dried out our things and sipped tea the rest of the afternoon. To the south, the north-facing slopes of the nearly 6000 meter peaks – including Lamo Angdang, the eastern most summit of the Kangchenjunga Group – were still heavily plastered with snow.

At dinner Pasang surprised us with a freshly baked cake with nuts and raisins. His Sherpa "oven" consisted of one pot nestled inside another with a handful of rocks separating the two. The cake was a culinary masterpiece, even though the bottom had been burnt. We wolfed it down as Pasang beamed with pride.

The weather held the next day, even though the dawn dragged ominous clouds across the eastern sky. We thought at first that it might snow.

Pat and I were eager to hit the trail and see Siniolchu up close for the first time. But the others lingered in a vain attempt to dry things out. Both Paul and RJ spread out all their gear on the blue tarp while the porters stood around watching and waiting for their loads.

Sickness also delayed us further. Leah was not feeling well. We did not know if her illness was due to the altitude or to a stomach bug. In spite of persistent nausea she elected to press on. Nima assigned her pack to one of the porters.

The trail climbed a steep, crumbling slope up to the lateral moraine of the rubble-strewn Zemu Glacier. Leah paused frequently to rest. The clouds soon evaporated. After topping another rise, we finally spied the mountain that had drawn us into northwestern Sikkim. Siniolchu, a dagger-like point of snow and ice, looked just as glorious and formidable as it did in Vittorio Sella's exquisite photographs. Pat pulled out his binoculars and studied the mountain's two ice falls intently.

In his day, Freshfield frankly judged the mountain to be unclimbable: "To us, Siniolchu seemed inaccessible!" he wrote. "For my own generation I am not afraid to use the word. But others will come, and, standing on our shoulders, will boast, as men did in Homer's day, that they are much better than their fathers. Who can tell?"

The "others" arrived in 1936. That is when a German team of four climbers led by the Bavarian Paul Bauer made the first ascent. Bauer had originally intended to scale Kangchenjunga via the northeast ridge. But when that attempt failed, he fell in love with the shapely Siniolchu. His team climbed its northwest ridge in fine, light-weight alpine style, establishing three camps along the way. After several tries, the two summiters, Karl Wien and Adi Göttner, made it to the top. Their triumph was short-lived: a year later both men died in an avalanche on Nanga Parbat.

The year after Bauer's success, a German-Swiss team claimed the second ascent, and a large Sikkimese-Indian team climbed it in 1976. In 1994 a fast-moving foursome of Slovenians put two on the summit. A year later two members of a "heavyweight" Japanese team of 13 led by Masafumi Katayama made the top. With any luck, ours would be the sixth ascent.

Six hours after leaving Yabuk, we arrived at the Siniolchu base camp. Pasang and the Sherpas had already established a kitchen by a low rock wall built by a previous expedition. As a welcoming gesture the Sherpas presented us with a cup of sweet milk tea and cookies as we looked around.

At 4570 meters base camp predictably was surrounded by austere ice, snow and rock. Yet the valley, dominated by the 30-kilometer-long Zemu Glacier, contained a rich network of life along its velvety green edges. Low-bush willows sprouted soft furry buds while dwarf rhododendrons held their tiny blossoms in tight clusters of colorful promise. Stunted juniper covered the rocky hillsides.

Birds of all description, most of which I regrettably could not name, found refuge here. They included long, sleek specimens with black wings and bright blue bodies, smaller fliers with bellies of mango and plainer sparrow-type song-birds. Flocks of snow pigeons pecked at the gravel until a disturbance caused them to rocket down the valley on swift wings. But my favorites were the choughs, a cousin of the raven. As soon as these pranksters discovered our camp, they scavenged for leftovers after every meal. With bright yellow beaks and red feet, they looked and acted like aerial clowns.

The camp was to be my home for the next two weeks. I had decided long before that I did not want to join Pat, Paul, Ace, Kit and Ali on the climb. Seeing the mountain up close confirmed the wisdom of my decision. I was more than happy to explore the surroundings.

A strong wind blew down the valley like a cold blast from the powerful lungs of Kangchenjunga. The mountain's great hulk loomed at the head of the Zemu Glacier less than 20 kilometers away. An alpine battalion of stalwart guards surrounded it: The Twins, Nepal Peak and Tent Peak, all named by Freshfield a century ago. Then the clouds moved in again, leaving us cloaked in a heavy Scottish-like mist. The sweltering heat of Delhi now seemed like a distant memory.

Pat awoke at 4:45 the next morning to photograph the sunrise. Kangchenjunga reflected the first swath of light. Then the summit flutings of Siniolchu glowed with the cross-lighting of the dawn. Within 15 minutes, a high overcast filled the sky and the pink colors hung there, muted. Pat wrote in his diary: "Having squinted through

the viewfinder off and on for a couple hours, I was blown away by the perfect pro-portions of this peak. From any angle, framed horizontally or vertically, it presents its best side to the camera."

Temba, who appeared to be the lowest in the pecking order among the five Sherpas, got things going each day. He wore a thin jacket over his pullover and a hand-knit wool hat popular with trekkers in Nepal. Today he made a smoky fire by throwing on some green juniper boughs. He stood over the thick smoke for a long time, finding purification and consolation in the morning ritual. The air was filled with its sweet fragrance – a scent I associate with many a Himalayan sojourn.

Nima, Ugen, Pat and I went for a stroll to Green Lake at the head of the valley. The jumbled creek boulders made walking difficult at first, but soon gave way to open grasslands. The trough continued in a gentle incline all the way. On the right it was confined by the steep slopes and on the left by a drop-off to the glacier some 50 meters below. The hike reminded us of a trail in Nepal up the Gokyo Valley where the 8000-meter peak of Cho Oyu plugs the far end of the valley.

Earlier that morning, Nima had spotted sheep tracks in the sand right beside base camp. So, we were not too surprised to find three ewes and a yearling lamb grazing on the lateral moraine. Ugen, on the other hand, shouted, "Look at the sheep!" Startled, they bounded like antelope across the grassy tufts and soon gained the steep slopes on the right, where they blended in perfectly with the colour of the rocks and soil. When I good-naturedly chided Ugen for shouting, he protested, "But I've never seen the bharal before."

We could now look back at Siniolchu – pointed and perfectly defined. Pat studied the final technical difficulties. "If we stick close to the rocky prominences, I think we can avoid the blue ice on the left side of the slope. And then maybe on the way down we can find cracks in the rocks to place anchors for rappelling," he thought aloud, anticipating the thrill of summit day.

Within two hours of leaving base camp, we arrived at a broad pasture by Green Lake, a muddy tarn that had been largely filled in by a mudslide. Freshfield described this grassy meadow rather humorously:

> It would make an excellent golf ground. For the golfer nothing is sacred. He exhib-its his skill unabashed under the shadow of the Pyramids. . . . Since the hillsides of

Sherpas Temba and Tendup uphold the British colonial tradition
of serving bed tea on our trek to Siniolchu base camp.

Darjiling [sic] are too steep for him, the day may come when in order to follow his fascinating pursuit he will resort to the back of Kangchenjunga, and argue over the respective charms of 'bunkers' and crevasses with the mountaineers of the coming century in a Club-hut beside the Zemu Glacier.

A stiff breeze picked up, and we headed back. At the spot where we sighted the blue sheep, Ugen again let out a whoop and pointed out a herd of 25 bharal further up the slope. I let out a yelp of my own as three rams battered at each other in mock combat.

Sangay, who had remained in Lachen to supervise the porters, now turned up with some more gear. He assured us the rest of the loads would arrive later, which meant another day's delay. He also brought news that the second liaison officer assigned to the expedition by the Ministry of Defense in Delhi would be arriving soon. We were not looking forward to his arrival.

The usual afternoon fog charged up the valley like a race horse sprinting for the

Team members (l to r) Kit Katzenbach, Ace Kvale, Paul Kallmes and Ali Palmer kick up their heels at base camp.

finish line. It moved so fast that I could feel it brushing against my cheek. Snow showers soon followed. Upon hearing Pasang's shrill whistle we dove into the dining tent for a bowl of soup. We sat, chattering away, revising our plans yet again, when the liaison officer straggled in, wet and miserable.

It had taken him five days to get here from Delhi, and we knew that he was probably suffering from the effects of climbing too high, too fast. In two days he marched the same trail from Lachen that had taken us four. His soaking wet nylon jacket clung to his skin like cellophane wrap, and his street shoes were sodden and icy. He barked out an order at Sangay to get his dry clothing out of his pack, but the Sherpa quickly disappeared to the cook tent.

Kit offered to lend him a hand, but he refused. "Let me introduce myself," he sputtered with a flourish of his arm. "I am Captain...." (His mouth was too frozen to enunciate properly and he muttered something unintelligible.) We offered him a seat, and he demanded a cup of tea. We sat there, sullen and deflated, disbelieving this intrusion into the tranquil Republic of Zemu.

"I am a fighter pilot," he explained after his face had thawed out a little. "I have been assigned to you for security reasons, you know." His helpless and hopeless appearance begged the question: what caliber of pilot would be taken off his regular duty and assigned to an inconsequential task such as this? We later learned that his name was V. V. Singh. "You can call me VV," he offered. But by that point, Paul had already christened him "Top Gun."

We got up early again the next morning to watch the dawn light up Kang-chenjunga. A huge lenticular cloud hovered perfectly over the summit like a flying saucer. Soon a second yet smaller cap formed on top of that one. Even from this distance we could see the winds tearing spindrift the peak as if trying to pry open the "Five Treasuries of Eternal Snow." Finally, the upper cloud dissipated as the lower one grew thicker, and our attention turned to Siniolchu.

Waist-deep snow immobilized Freshfield's expedition near Siniolchu, and that event gave the explorer much time to reflect on the mountain:

> We gazed with ceaseless delight on the peak immediately opposite our camp –
> Siniolchum [sic], 22,570 feet – the most beautiful mountain I have ever seen, perhaps
> the most beautiful in the world. Its icy sides are exquisitely fluted by avalanches; the

snow upon its edges is blown up into fantastic fringes, as thin as to be transparent in the Indian sunshine. It is the embodiment of the Inaccessible, a fitting throne for the Spirits of the Summits.

Since catching our first glimpse of "the Inaccessible" we had admired the prow of ice and snow that splits the steep north face. "This is surely a plum ripe for plucking by a bold team," announced Pat. Fate had other plans. A serac, a tower of ice, abruptly collapsed at the top of that route, sending a huge avalanche billowing off the face. An awesome snow cloud covered the lower ice fall in powder.

"Scratch that one off the list, at least for this team," Pat concluded.

After breakfast the final contingent of porters arrived from Yabuk. They wasted no time in lingering since they wanted to make it back to Lachen by evening. They dumped their loads and grabbed a cup of tea. Nima insisted that we examine our duffel bags to make sure nothing was missing. Then he checked off the porters' names in his book. We watched the Lachen gang scamper down the valley in their blue-and-red boots like children skipping in a playground.

As it turned out we needed an extra day to prepare our things for the climb. The others fussed about adjusting crampons and repackaging food – all small detail work that could have been done at home. The altitude slowed everyone down.

"Don't forget I'm a sea level desk jockey," Paul beseeched.

Leah was still sick. The malaise that had struck her a few days ago had not improved. We asked Ugen and one of the Sherpas to take her down to a lower elevation to see if she would recover. After all the permit trouble it took to include her on the team, it seemed ironic that she would be the first to leave. After a round of farewell hugs and encouragement, we watched her walk down the valley. As it turned out, her illness persisted. Ugen eventually escorted her all the way back to Gangtok and then Bagdogra, where he put her on a flight to Calcutta.

Top Gun, on the other hand, recovered. He hovered around us like a dark, nagging cloud as we sorted our gear. Having never climbed a mountain he freely offered advice on the route as well as the proper way to drink imported whiskey. At a cocktail party in Delhi we might have been humored by him. But here his arrogant airs were grossly out of place.

I took the prayer flags I bought in Gangtok down to the kitchen and asked the

A herd of bharal (blue sheep) graze on the hillsides within the boundaries of Sikkim's Kangchenjunga National Park.

Sherpas if we could put them up. "Today is not a good day," replied Nima who knew about these kinds of things. "We'll do it tomorrow before we go on the mountain."

By early evening we had all retreated to our tents. From the darkness I heard Pasang exude one final prayer: *Om mani padme hum.* Hail to the Jewel in the Lotus. The blessing wafted into the quiet of the night.

Snow bridges, created by massive avalanches, span the Zemu River during our four-day trek to base camp.

Chapter 3

FOOTSTEPS IN THE CLOUDS

Base Camp, May 4, 1998

Across the Zemu Valley, the pointed peak of Siniolchu now beckoned. My newly hung prayer flags flapped in the breeze, and Nima tossed green juniper boughs onto the fire in a final prayer for the climbers. Under the hollow-eyed gaze of two bleached sheep skulls mounted on a kitchen pole, the expedition left base camp. RJ, Nima, Sangay, Temba and I acted as the gear shuttle service in order to help the climbers establish their first camp.

The rocky rubble of the Zemu Glacier tenaciously guarded the base of Siniolchu. But sporadic cairns from the 1995 Japanese expedition helped guide us through the chaos. Teetering boulders, slippery mud and soft snow demanded all of our concentration and focus. As we Westerners plodded on like lumbering elephants, the Sherpas scampered from rock to rock like swift-footed sheep.

After a four-and-a-half-hour hike, we found a perfect site for Camp 1. (In reality the point served as an advanced base camp because the mountain began several hundred meters above that point.) The spot straddled a three-meter-wide fin of ice flanked by gaping crevasses. Most importantly, it lay protected from avalanches under a granite prow that soared into the sky like a giant cleaver. A nearby hollow in the ice

As Freshfield's group tried to circumnavigate Kangchenjunga's north side a big snowstorm, that dumped two meters of snow on the ground, nearly forced them to turn back. PHOTO: VITTORIO SELLA

OVERLEAF. *Mt. Siniolchu, described by Douglas Freshfield as the "most beautiful mountain in the world," soars to 6887 meters just 19 kilometers to the east of Kangchenjunga.*

formed a perfect receptacle for melted snow, a water source that helped save on fuel consumption.

After unloading the gear I bade the climbers, Ace, Kit, Paul and Ali farewell. I had a lump in my throat as I hugged Pat and managed only a fleeting good bye. I tried hard not to be a worrying spouse. But with its hanging glaciers and crumbling ice falls, Siniolchu looked hard and dangerous. Pat, of course, longed to be on a big mountain again where he could enjoy the sensation of living in the extraordinary world between earth and sky.

Nima told us that, "Mind should be clear when climbing. If too many other things to worry about, then not clear. Then no good." On Siniolchu Pat had to focus singularly on just one thing: the mountain. I turned around and retreated to base camp. The climb was now up to Pat and his teammates. His diary reads:

May 5, Camp 1: I sensed from the very beginning that the mountain was grossly out of shape. The mushy snow on the lower Siniolchu Glacier was the first sign that much trouble lay ahead. It forced us to wallow and grovel upward.

"Well, we can thank El Niño for this," said Paul, as sweat cascaded from his forehead and splashed onto his chest. To our chagrin, his thermometer shot past 30 degrees Celsius in the direct sun. At the same time, all of northern India was reeling under its worst heat wave in 50 years. Temperatures peaked in some lowland regions at a smoldering 51 degrees Celsius. According to newspaper reports, the heat spell killed more than 2,300 people that spring.

But as we left Camp 1 at 4:30 A.M., I was totally psyched to scale Siniolchu. We planned to follow the

TOP TO BOTTOM: *Paul Kallmes, Ace Kvale, Sangay Sherpa with a chough.*

route first tackled by Bauer's team. But in order to reach the long and complicated summit ridge, we had to pass through two icefalls. Put together, these crevasse-ridden features roughly equaled the length of the Khumbu Icefall that bars the way to the upper slopes of Everest.

In preparing for the climb, I had spent much of the winter scaling frozen waterfalls or ski mountaineering in the Canadian Rockies. In all fairness to one's partners, there is really only one basic protocol for coming on a serious climb like this: getting in shape for the rigors of slogging uphill, under immense loads, in an atmosphere that offers less than half the oxygen at sea level.

This morning I felt at the top of my form as I led the others into the darkness. Being the grizzled "stair master" with the most experience slogging up big mountains, I felt obliged to break trail and negotiate most of the way through the first icefall. The others followed, roped together, with heavier loads. At this altitude, between 5000 and 5700 meters, there had been no freezing cycle since the last major storm. Now with every step we plunged up to our shins in heavy, isothermic snow, which soaked right through our waterproof gaiters.

After checking with the team, I picked a circuitous line that zigged and zagged up a series of snow ramps, weaving amongst a forest of ice towers. To my surprise we came across a set of tracks, possibly those of a fox, that had wandered through here a day or two before. The sun had almost effaced them. "What had this animal been looking for?" I wondered. Most likely something more tangible than what we were after.

Further up we found more evidence of life on the mountain. A five-meter section of rope protruded near the top of the upper ramp, a remnant from the large Japanese team. To make things a lot easier for themselves the Japanese employed Sherpas to secure 2,000 meters of fixed line in the two ice falls. While the trend in mountaineering these days supports lightweight, self-sufficient climbs, such old-style "siege" tactics still prevail. Everest is still retro-fitted with a convenient rope "handrail" and a series of ladders from bottom to top to facilitate the climb. The only tool an Everest "climber" needs on the regular South Col route now is a jumar, a metal ascending device that slides one way up a rope.

I wanted to do this climb in a simple, self-reliant manner – to "give the mountain a chance," as top alpinist Reinhold Messner once said – just as I would back home. That meant climbing without the help of Sherpas and with limited gear. By traveling light we would also lessen our impact on the environment.

We needed to use our crampons only once on a short traverse. I led out across the 45-degree ramp of ice, burying my arms up to the elbows in slush. I augured in three ice screws to secure a 30-meter length of rope. I hoped it might safeguard our passage through this section over the next few days while carrying loads. By the time we descended an hour later, the searing rays of the sun had already melted out one of the screws. I plugged it back in, knowing that it offered more psychological back-up than real protection.

As we descended, I could see the tiny figures of Baiba, RJ and the Sherpas dropping a second load for us at Camp 1 far below. They stood there for some time, no doubt offering moral support to Kit, who was feeling sick. Tall and athletic, Kit was a competitive mountain runner. But she was not used to being sidelined by little things like an ailing stomach. "I usually find a 50 kilometer run more difficult than a climb. But here I am incapacitated and there's nothing I can do to fight this stomach bug," she moaned.

We made it back to Camp 1 just after 12:00 P.M. A major slush avalanche originating 1,000 meters above us had covered our tracks with truckloads of snow. Back at the tent and somewhat shaken by the magnitude of the debris, Ali posed some good questions. "We need to do something to lessen our chances of being hit," said the former climbing instructor. "Maybe we should think about beginning our days earlier – a lot earlier – when cooler temperatures will help stabilize the slopes."

We mulled over the suggestion. Taking this unsavory but necessary step would turn our climb into a nocturnal one. But we knew that this was the only solution. We then decided to reinvent our meal times and catch our deepest sleep early in the evening, between seven and midnight. We, the citizens of the newly formed Zemu Republic, would adapt to "Siniolchu mountain time."

The avalanche hazard now preoccupied us as the sun turned the mountain into a steam bath. On Kit's insistence, we had brought avalanche transceivers. "This is an expedition, not a vacation," she had said, emphasizing the seriousness of the endeavor. Now it took no reminders for everyone to wear them. Yet, given the magnitude of some of the avalanches on the mountain, survival under tons of snow seemed unlikely, with or without transceivers.

May 6: My alarm awoke me with a depressing thudding noise. It was midnight. I glanced out in groggy disorientation and saw the heavy fog muffling the starlight. Light snow fell with a hissing sound on our tent. The air was moist – a prime avalanche warning. Our headlamps cast eerie shadows through the darkness as we discussed the weather, tent to tent. We decided to call it a rest day, even though we had been on the mountain for only three days.

Big mountain climbing is as much a waiting game as a test of skill. One is always calculating how much food, fuel and patience can be used up while biding bad weather days. Thanks to these less-than-ideal circumstances, I was laid up in my sleeping bag preoccupied with such thoughts. On the other hand, being trapped in a tent is a great opportunity to get caught up on reading or daydreaming.

Now, my mind dwelled on avalanches. I began to wonder if we should have paid more attention to mountaineer Frank Smythe's comment that "May was the avalanche month." We had tried to schedule the expedition for the previous fall, but the Indian Mountaineering Federation had postponed that permit. The monsoon, which begins in early to mid-June, brings rain to the foothills and snow to the mountains. Nevertheless, two of the confirmed ascents after Bauer's successful bid had taken place in the spring.

The sun roasted us inside our tents all day. The bacon-grease heat, now manufacturing a cycle of sun, fog and sleet, forced me and my tent-mate Paul to stuff a sleeping bag against the ceiling to block the heat. Through the door, I passively watched a barrage of avalanches gushing down a slope little more than 100 meters to the east of our camp. Mount Siniolchu appeared to be oozing white detritus from suppurating wounds.

By noon the fog thickened and light snow started falling again. We slowly added more layers of clothing. At times, the booming of avalanches arrived in stereo, bouncing off either side of the valley. The solar heat combined with the sound effects started to wear on our nerves.

Seeking solace and a diversion, I clump-clumped in my unlaced plastic boots over to the tent that Ace, Kit and Ali shared. We feebly tried to raise each other's spirits with jokes about the weather. Ace laughed a little and then gave up. "Sorry, I'm fresh out of weather jokes."

OVERLEAF. *After a midnight carry to Camp 2, to avoid the heat of the sun, we descend the Siniolchu Glacier at dawn.*

May 7: The sky finally cleared and the temperature dropped just enough to firm up the snow. We had set the alarm for 11 P.M. to allow for an even earlier departure. In anticipation, I had prepared a Thermos flask of hot chocolate before going to sleep. Paul and I needed this welcome kick-start while preparing breakfast.

From my climbing experience with Sherpas, I have gotten into the habit of eating the same foods that sustain them. *Tsampa,* a roasted ground barley that is the staple of many Himalayan people, gives plenty of energy and is easy to digest at any altitude. While the Tibetans and Sherpas mix it in with *solja,* their salted, butter tea, I like it best with a spoonful of sugar and a wad of butter. Sometimes I even add a bit of hot chocolate powder.

The rank smell of kerosene, however, greatly spoiled our meals and our gusto for eating. White camping gas or a mixture of butane and propane is preferable for cooking because neither smells and each burns well. But in India kerosene is the only fuel available. Kerosene is finicky to use at the best of times. Here at higher altitudes it was barely flammable and required special priming. Kit's way of lighting her stove involved burning a twist of toilet paper close to the fuel opening of the burner for a minute. I dubbed this innovation the "Katzenbach Method." The smell and taste of kerosene permeated our clothing, sleeping bags and food. I never got used to it.

Around midnight the five of us headed out into the night. We followed our tracks by the narrow light of our headlamps. The only sound in the darkness came from the crunching of boots through the snow. No one was in the mood for talking. We arrived at our cache at 4:30 A.M. and dropped our loads of food and other gear. The stack of extra warm clothing I had brought in anticipation of the cold temperatures had now become superfluous in the heat.

As we descended, the pre-dawn light bathed the lower icefall in a lush blue cast. The high humidity created a richness of hue that I have rarely seen in other mountain settings. But it did not last long. We descended into a fog bank and arrived back at Camp 1 two hours later. Around midday the sky cleared and I hopped out of the solarium-like tent nude. I could not resist splashing slushy snow all over my body. The impromptu bath made my skin tingle and considerably lifted my spirits. "We're gonna climb this bastard!" I yelled to Paul who remained motionless inside the tent.

"Right," he hollered back, "and let's make short work of it!"

Paul, who had been feeling sick since our arrival at Camp 1, was not acclimatizing well. The tent was quickly becoming his prison and the mountain his nemesis. After all the effort he had put into planning this expedition, he could now do little more than lie still. In addition to stomach cramps and irregular breathing, he was dealing with the unpleasant side effects of acetazolamide, or Diamox. The drug is regularly taken to curb the debilitating effects of high altitude. His doctor had recommended the drug to prevent complications and further damage arising from a retinal hemorrhage he had suffered by walking into a door some six months ago. Although the Diamox kept the dilation of his retina in check, it had unfortunate side-effects. Paul now felt the typical tingling sensations in his fingers, lips and toes.

I could both identify and sympathize with Paul's plight. In 1996 I was on an expedition to the Sichuan Himalaya in China. There I picked up a severe respiratory bug in the filthy city of Chengdu. It kept me from joining my companions in their attempt to make the first ascent of a 6000-meter peak called Jamyang that rivals Siniolchu for beauty. Ultimately, my fellow climbers were turned back just a day's climb from the top simply because they had not allowed enough time for acclimatization.

May 8: I was getting used to the routine now. Up at midnight and off by 2 A.M. Today we planned to move our tents to the site of Camp 2. I was relieved to see that Kit was gaining strength. At the toe of the glacier we paused for a drink and put on harnesses and uncoiled the ropes. Through the otherwise cloyingly gray light, I noticed an intense pinpoint glow emanating from a peak in the east. I immediately thought of *Shambhala,* a heavenly sanctuary on earth that Tibetans talk about. After some time I realized the phenomenon was nothing more than a finger of sunlight that had managed to poke its way through a wall of cloud choking the sky. Another flight of fancy brought back to earth.

We found a spot for Camp 2 that was relatively protected from avalanche slopes. We assumed that the soggy snow pack near our camp would probably stop any ice chunks falling off the face of Siniolchu. The mountain's immense north face and its gleaming pendants of hanging glaciers felt like they were directly above us. In reality it was still half a kilometer away.

I now realized that any hope of climbing a new route to the top would have to wait until another season and another climbing team. Avalanches blocked the obvious alternative – a direct climb on the north face.

OVERLEAF. *Camp 2 below the north face of Mt. Siniochu. The original route winds through the second icefall (on right), then follows the summit ridge to the top.*

As the midday fog rolled in we resumed our customary horizontal position on the melting mountain. From the depths of his sleeping bag the ailing Paul jokingly called us a bunch of "tent potatoes."

May 9, Camp 2: We made this a rest-and-acclimatization day. Ali and I went for an hour's stroll with binoculars in hand to try to scope a route through the upper icefall to our next and final camp. We angled up the slope, enjoying the support given by a veneer of hard snow that had formed. From what we could see there seemed to be only two choices of route. One was to skirt the icefall on the right side, forcing our way up a vertical trough beside a rock rib threatened by rotten seracs. The other option was to take a zigzag approach in the middle on steep ice ramps beneath intimidating seracs almost twice as high as those in the lower icefall. Neither route looked very appealing.

The super-saturated condition of the snow provided us with one, and only one, unexpected blessing. The snow was so waterlogged that it needed little melting for cooking. This boosted fuel efficiency and decreased our consumption of kerosene by at least a third. On the down side, the condition of the snow made it too dangerous to continue, although I did not want to admit that just yet.

Nevertheless, our resolve to climb remained strong. After traveling such a great distance we wanted to push ourselves as hard as safety allowed. On a Canadian mountain beset with similar bad snow conditions I would have retreated right away and returned only when the weather and snow conditions improved. But here the ticking clock of the impending monsoon kept us pushing. Our permit did not allow time for second attempts.

May 10: While Paul stayed at camp, the rest of us shouldered heavy loads and headed into the darkness. Paul had been suffering from apnea and was sleeping poorly. "Every time I lie down," he said, "I feel like I might suffocate." This unnerving sensation forced him to sit upright, gasping for air. He dozed fitfully by propping himself upright against his pack and now resigned himself to abandoning the climb. I secretly hoped his condition did not deteriorate into an emergency evacuation.

In the limbo of pre-dawn, it was hard to find the route to the foot of the icefall Ali and I had reconnoitered. Daylight came to our rescue just as we reached an ascending snow ramp. A gompa-sized serac loomed above us. Kit went first. With ice axes in hand and crampons on her feet, she forged the way up a three-meter-high vertical wall. Then Ace tackled the final 25-meter section across an exposed drop-off of more than 50 meters. Once established at the top of the pitch, they threw down the rope to me and Ali. We tied into it and followed safely with our heavy packs.

By now the sun had burned through the damp fog, and the mercury began to rise. At first we luxuriated in the warmth, sitting quietly, nibbling a snack. But the rising heat and collapsing snow soon became our task masters, urging us to descend quickly. The effort it took to plod through the heavy snow made each day feel like a summit day. With or without a pack, every move in the thin air exhausted us.

Before turning back, Ali and I struck off to look for a route through the second icefall. My rope partner was slightly built but a powerhouse nonetheless. Her mild-mannered disposition, nurtured by wells of patience, helped keep our group dynamics on an even keel. My own approach to problem-solving was to do the boy thing, and plunge into silence. No matter the challenge, Ali was the first to verbalize it.

Kit Katzenbach climbs below towering seracs through the second icefall. The unseasonably hot temperatures turned the ice into rotten honeycombs that threatened to crumble on top of us.

It was apparent to both the silent and the verbal that Siniolchu really offered no safe way up. After stepping gingerly over a decayed snow bridge that spanned a dark-throated crevasse, we came up against two parallel crevasses. We could see our goal, the top of the glacier, a tantalizing 20 meters above us. But the ice wall looked like a rotten honeycomb. Even if we could get up this disastrous configuration and secure a fixed line to aid up and down passage, the anchors would melt out and we would have to go through the same absurdly dangerous moves again and again. I did not like the look of it at all.

The size of the seracs and the crevasses on this route up Siniolchu reminded me of the Khumbu Icefall on Everest in 1982. At the time, snow conditions had been perfect for fixing ropes and ladders through a maze of 20-meter high ice towers and deep crevasses. Thanks to overnight sub-zero temperatures the snow had a Styrofoam crispness, and properly placed anchors never melted out. But I had still been very scared. I had to pass through that dangerous "bowling alley" five or six times times in each direction, conscious of the possibility of being snuffed by collapsing ice every time. Two weeks into the expedition, three Sherpas were buried and killed in an

Our high point midway up the second icefall at 5670 meters, looking towards Tibet.

74

avalanche. Two days after that a serac crumbled and crushed one of my teammates, Blair Griffiths. I did not want any such memories from Siniolchu.

Ali and I hesitated. The snow had the consistency of whipped cream. The ice wall we had to climb up resembled soft Swiss cheese. In short, the smorgasbord ahead of us looked very unappetizing. At this stage of my life, I wanted to limit my exposure to unnecessary risk.

As we looked furtively for a way to reach the upper icefall, the sun's rays continued its eroding work. The steep serac walls around us greatly amplified the heat. As a consequence the early morning crisp surface was now mush. We returned to where Ace and Kit waited and reported our findings.

We rigged a rappel with two aluminum snow flukes as anchors, and then took turns, warily backing off. With our energy ebbing quickly we traced our steps downward, frequently plunging into snow above our knees. I recoiled at the thought of diving head first into one of dozens of gaping crevasses that we had unwittingly avoided in the early hours in the weak light of our headlamps.

At the snout of the icefall we stashed our loads in heavy plastic bags. At this point we were still determined to return for another try. The four of us then wallowed back to camp. The porridge-like snow forced us to crawl on hands and knees like infants learning to walk.

Paul who had languished in boredom and frustration at the camp now greeted us with excitement. "Way to go. I saw you reach your high point!" We related our tribulations and fears about the condition of the route.

"Come on, you guys. If Bauer's dog Wastl could make it to Camp 3 – no ropes, no crampons – then surely we can do it," Paul chided us good naturedly. It was true. When Bauer's team climbed Siniolchu, a village dog had followed them all the way to base camp and then high onto the mountain. But judging from the photos in Bauer's book, *Himalayan Quest,* the upper icefall looked nothing like the jumbled mess of ice we were encountering more than 50 years later. On their summit day, Göttner and Wien had put in a stellar effort, using their innate skills as climbers to tread where no others had been. The dog Wastl made what must have been the canine high-altitude record if its day.

Global warming has played havoc with mountain ice around the world. While climbing Everest I found that the condition of the Khumbu Icefall had changed remarkably since Hillary and Tenzing's climb 30 years earlier. While Hillary's team had used only one ladder (a tree trunk) to span the crevasses, we required 60 aluminum ones to cross the tortured chaos of ice. Although it is not common to carry ladders on any but the biggest mountains, just two might have changed the outcome of our expedition here on Siniolchu.

In the afternoon, a snow squall threatened to trap us indefinitely on the mountain. I nestled into my sleeping bag to read about the adventures of the prolific British mountaineer Bill Tilman. On his return from an attempt on Everest in 1938, Tilman and two Sherpas investigated the gap between Mounts Siniolchu and Simvu as a possible shortcut back to Darjeeling. They left Green Lake and crossed the Zemu Glacier, climbing continuously to the high pass.

Near the top of the glacier they came upon the tracks of a person, or so they thought. With considerable difficulty they used a rope to descend the steep and treacherous Tongshyong Glacier and made their way back to Darjeeling via Dzongri. Curious about the origin of the tracks, Tilman inquired whether other mountaineer-

Mt. Siniolchu after the big snow storm. PHOTO: VITTORIO SELLA

ing parties were in the area, and found there were none. Having seen a similar set of tracks on the Biafo Glacier in the Karakorum the previous year, he deduced, only partly in jest, that they might belong to the *yeti*, or abominable snowman.

With my thoughts partially lost in Tilman's adventures, I waited for the storm to run its course. In the first few hours more than 12 centimeters of snow accumulated. In my 21 years of expedition climbing, I had never seen a more concerted effort by a mountain to thwart an expedition.

May 11: The storm continued and the whoosh and boom of avalanches charging down Siniolchu's north face kept me on edge. For nearly an hour at midday, when the sun was near its zenith above the clouds, an avalanche crashed down the mountain every five minutes.

In mid-afternoon, as I lay dozing, a deafening thunderclap echoed throughout the mountain arena. Electricity charged the air. Ace's hair bizarrely stood on end when he went outside to clear snow from the tent walls. Whenever the white-hot fog parted, the mountain glared down at us, haughty and wild. The full moon rose unnoticed somewhere above the gloom.

I woke up in the middle of the night with a fantasy of climbing the mountain with only Ace. The two of us had the most high-altitude climbing experience, and I thought that we might make it to the top with just a small bivvy tent and enough food and fuel for three days. Perhaps if we stuck our necks out we could successfully run the gauntlet of teetering seracs in the upper icefall. The relative inexperience of my other team members now frustrated me. As the oldest on the expedition by several years (and almost a full 20 older than Kit) I now realized how much I had previously depended on more experienced climbers to call the shots.

May 12: Feeling thoroughly humbled by the savagery of the weather, we held an impromptu meeting in our tents. Uncertainty and danger faced us all around. We had no way of knowing if another storm was on the way. Nor could we count on a cooling trend to stabilize the 35 centimeters of powder now sitting on top of the mush. Even if it did get cold, it would take much longer to consolidate the snow than our food supplies would last.

In the end it was obvious. We decided to play it safe and retreat. Beneath

OVERLEAF. *A lenticular cloud forms over Kangchenjunga, signaling high winds, at the head of the Zemu Valley.*

Siniolchu's grace and loveliness lay a spirit of open resistance. The mountain would abide no more visitors this spring. As Ace pointed out, "To wait out this bad weather we would have to go down to base camp because we don't have enough food up here. Dammit. The red tape in Delhi and Gangtok seriously cut into whatever extra time we had in our schedule."

The four of us retrieved the gear we had stashed at the icefall and toiled back down through the deep snow to our tents. In the harsh reality of daylight, my fantasy about making a dash for the summit seemed foolhardy.

May 13: I stuck my head out of the tent and was relieved to see clear, blue sky. Cold air hung in the stillness. The scene was both soothing and invigorating. Mercifully, not more than three or four avalanches crashed down.

We had a lengthy discussion about how nature and luck had dealt us a less-than-perfect hand of cards. "This is a much more committing route than I had originally thought," reflected Ace. "The complicated approach through the two ice falls just to get to the summit ridge makes it feel like a much higher mountain. And the `sting' comes at the very end, where the final ridge sharpens into a knife edge with a 45-degree slab of snow and ice. Man, just look at that summit!"

We all looked up for the umpteenth time. For the past week, the summit and its long, challenging ridge had looked tantalizingly close. Images of just how close we had come would haunt me for the next several weeks.

But now my thoughts turned to salvaging the trip. We still harbored a secondary goal of reaching Nepal Gap, which would complete our first half-circle around Kangchenjunga. To do so would mean retreating to base camp, resting a day, then packing and heading further up the Zemu Valley. But in Darjeeling, Dorjee Lhatoo had told us the trek to Nepal Gap would take four days round-trip. I now wondered if we would have enough time to get to the Gap. Our permits were due to expire only a few days after that, and we still had a two-day hike to Lachen. How lucky Paul Bauer and his group had been when they ascended Siniolchu. They had no problems with permits or politics and had the luxury of remaining in the area over a five-week period before they finally reached the top on a third attempt. That kind of freedom no longer exists in the Sikkim Himalaya.

With little ceremony we made the hard decision to abandon the mountain and commit to Plan B – reaching Nepal Gap. Our immediate task at hand now was to remove all our gear and garbage from the mountain. It was a magical morning as the steel-blue light of dawn licked the east side of the seracs, and an opaque moonlight filled in the shadow side. The ghostly images of these seracs resembled snow-plastered *juho,* or "ghost-trees" I had once seen while ski touring in Japan.

We meticulously cleared our camps and headed towards the Zemu Valley. Whatever did not fit into our backpacks now filled garbage bags that we lowered ahead of us on a rope leash as we descended. We looked like dog owners out for a stroll. But this was no walk in the park. We had a tough time breaking trail, even downhill. A thick crust on top of powder snow would not support body weight. At every step our front-end man, Ace, broke through the crust, banging his shins against the hard layer while floundering in the loose underlying snow. Paul ambled behind. Once freed from his high altitude hospital ward he gained strength with each downward stride.

As we straggled into base camp, only Pasang and Nima greeted us. RJ had left that morning, escorted by Tendup, to catch a flight home. Baiba had hiked part way with them to try and get a better view of our position on the mountain. I sat sipping tea in the warm sun with Nima, who jokingly offered me an energy bar. "Thanks Nima, but I'd rather have a yak burger," I retorted. Tucked into the sweet-smelling greenery of juniper and rhododendron ground cover along the moraine, the base camp looked more hospitable than I remembered.

When Baiba came back she seemed startled to see me, and broke into tears. After not seeing any sign of us on the mountain, she had begun to think that something had happened to us. She, too, had heard the ominous thunderclap that had reverberated during the big storm. We embraced, long and hard, and brought each other up to date with our stories.

"I don't think I like being a base camp groupie, after all," she said after her heaving sobs calmed down. "But I did have fun, especially after VV left." The irritating liaison officer had quit base camp a week ago, complaining of a sore tooth. "It was like a black cloud had moved on," said Baiba. We would later meet him in Gangtok where he had been staying at an expensive hotel, at our expense.

May 14: Paul woke up refreshed and bright-eyed, having slept a full seven hours. That was more sleep, he said, than he ever got the entire time on the mountain. But his disappointment at his personal performance soured his conscience like a mouthful of curdled milk. He was now keen to get the hell out. Instead of reveling for a few more days in the beauty of the Zemu Valley – a place we would probably never see again due to the high costs – Paul only talked about returning to the States. With Ugen and Tendup accompanying him, he hefted his pack and strode down the valley like a man with a mission.

None of us shared Paul's compulsion to leave Sikkim. Although thwarted by the mountain, we were still hungry to see more than just the inside of a storm-bound tent. It did not take long to plan and sort our gear for a lightweight foray to Nepal Gap. We had three days to make the trip before the porters were due to come from Lachen. Now well acclimatized to the altitude we reckoned we could made the trip quickly. Baiba decided to stay back, although she, Nima and Temba would help to carry our gear up past Green Lake.

May 17: Ace, Ali, Kit and I left our camp on the Nepal Gap Glacier at 3 A.M., a half-moon lighting our way. The trek covered 10 kilometers and gained 1,000 meters. The climb looked a bit like the King Trench route on Canada's highest peak, Mount Logan. But Nepal Gap, at an elevation of 6000 meters, was 40 meters higher than Logan's summit.

The snow surface was firm, allowing us to plod right up the middle of the broad plain of the glacier. We had a rope handy but we did not need it now. We would use it upon our return eight hours later when the sun had weakened the surface tension of the snow, increasing the danger of falling into a crevasse.

From a distance the gentle terrain appeared to lead to the col. As such I was suckered into leaving a stash of clothing and my crampons for retrieval on the way back. But as we approached, I regretted my decision to leave the crampons behind. A rocky headwall broken only in a couple places stretched in a jagged inverse arc between Nepal Peak and the easternmost of the 7000-meter-high Twins. My companions kicked steps for 100 meters on steep snow to the right before scrambling the rest of the way on broken rock. My only alternative was to investigate a steep gully which featured great loose blocks of gray granite cemented together by ice. With skills honed on the crumbly limestone of my native Canadian Rockies, I gingerly worked my way up the jagged furrow, being careful to pull down, and not out, on the handholds.

Within 20 meters the gully eased off and I was able to scramble onto a slope stacked with small boulders to the crest of the col. There I awaited my teammates. The first glimpse westward into Nepal was breathtaking. The slopes plunged even steeper down that side. Immediately to the south, the huge relief of the north faces of the Twins reared up above the ridge. The hazy bulk of sacred Chomolhari, the throne of the goddess Dorje Phagmo, shimmered in the distance in Bhutan.

Siniolchu, a slender dancer frozen in a pirouette, teased me in the full sunlight of day. Kangchenjunga, anything but graceful, squatted on powerful haunches of snow at the head of the Zemu Glacier.

The others duly arrived, and Ali uttered her favorite declaration, "Here we are then."

Nepal Gap proved to be my summit on this expedition. I knew that I would chew hard on the disappointment of Siniolchu, but at this moment, perched on the edge of Nepal and Sikkim, that did not matter. There would be other opportunities and other mountains. Now, all that remained was to return home, back to the other side of the earth, and prepare for the second half of the journey.

Our expedition ended with a climb up to Nepal Gap (out of sight to the left) on the border with Nepal and Sikkim. Tent Peak is on the right and Nepal Peak on the left.

Chapter 4
ON THE WINGS OF BUDDHA

Kathmandu, October 28, 1998

IN KATHMANDU IT IS HARD TO ESCAPE THE SPECTER OF EVEREST. Although the world's highest mountain physically lies 180 kilometers from Nepal's capital, its commercial equivalents beckon everywhere: Everest Express Trekking, Everest Toothpaste, Everest Solvent, Everest Whiskey, Everest Sheraton Hotel, Everest Water Treatment Systems – even the Everest College Cricket Coaching Academy.

Not surprisingly, Everest, the global celebrity, dominated the news as Pat and I arrived in the ancient city in October. One billboard even congratulated Kaji Sherpa and his Tuborg beer-sponsored "Speed Everest Expedition" for his recent world record 20-hour-and-24-minute ascent. City newspapers also celebrated the Taiwanese photographer and returning Everest hero known as Makalu Gau. Front page photos showed Gau clutching his camera with what remained of his amputated hands. The photographer lost his fingers and toes during his ascent in May 1996 (his summit partner was not so lucky and died during the attempt). A total of 12 climbers perished on the world's highest mountain that month. Now every other person sitting in a Kathmandu café, it seemed, was dutifully reading about the fiasco in Jon Krakauer's book, *Into Thin Air*.

A mixture of the sacred and the profane at Bodhnath, Kathmandu.

But as the world obsessed about Everest, we made our final arrangements to go to Kangchenjunga. Like Everest it remains "one of the glories of the world." But unlike the "Big E," Kangchenjunga has yet to be commercially exploited. For us the mountain's sacred character combined with its relative obscurity was all part of its attractiveness.

Ravi Chandra, a friend who owns the trekking agency AmaDablam Adventure Group, handled the logistics and official paperwork for the expedition. Compared to the bureaucratic hurdles we faced to get to the northeast side of Kangchenjunga in Sikkim, the Nepali formalities were a breeze. In recent years Nepal's Central Immigration Office of the Home Ministry has, much to its credit, streamlined the permit process for trekking and climbing permits.

Even so, Ravi offered our group of Canadian trekkers some sensible advice. "When you come to Nepal, time is stretchable," he said with a knowing smile. In other words, western concepts of order and reality mean little in a country where a mind-boggling array of thousand-armed deities and demon-slaying goddesses can play havoc with everyday life. With a shrug of their shoulders Nepalis typically face calamities and hardships by fatalistically muttering "*Ke garne?*" It means, roughly, "Shit happens, what to do?" It is as good a motto as any for Himalayan travelers.

Pat and I well understood Nepal's infinitely expandable "mountain time." In total we have spent nearly a year trekking or climbing in Nepal. But for the rest of our party Nepal's idiosyncrasies were largely a new experience.

Our friend Margie Jamieson half expected the Himalaya to be an Asian version of "Twomey Time." For the last 20 years she and her partner, Art Twomey, had lived in the Purcell Mountain Range near Pat's home town of Kimberley, British Columbia. Born with the gift of the gab, Art was usually late for engagements, thus earning a reputation during his free-wheeling life for operating on "Twomey Time." But up in the Purcells, where Art and Margie's popular ski guiding business called Ptarmigan Tours took hold, "Twomey Time" was part of the attraction.

When Art died in a helicopter crash in January of 1997, Margie continued to run the ever-busy business. But she admitted that the death drove home to her the urgency of not waiting too long to do the important things in life. She had always wanted to see the Himalaya.

We all missed Art very much. He had been the single most influential person in Pat's early life and had convinced Pat of the feasibility of making a living as a freelance photographer. Art also had great stories to tell about Nepal. In 1977 he and a small team of Kiwis tackled Everest via the South Col route. Unlike most of the expeditions before or since, they used no Sherpas to carry loads on the mountain. Their summit attempt failed when bad weather forced them back just hours from the top.

Like Margie, our other three companions were Himalaya neophytes. They included Ilana Cameron, the 20-year-old daughter of Margie's close friends from Vancouver; Dave Quinn, a strapping back-country skier and hiker with a biology background from Kimberley, British Columbia, and Davin Macintosh, a keen athlete from Canmore, Alberta who had recently retired from a cross-country ski racing career.

All had come to experience Nepal and, in the process, help us retrace the journey taken by Douglas Freshfield and Vittorio Sella. At the time of their Kangchenjunga circuit one hundred years ago, Nepal remained very much a forbidden domain. Ruled by a king believed to be a reincarnation of the benevolent Hindu god, Vishnu, Nepal kept its doors closed to foreigners for centuries: to avoid contamination from the spurious ways of the outside world. Until the late 1940s no more than 226 outsiders had visited Nepal.

To tour around Kangchenjunga Freshfield's party began in Darjeeling and headed east, then northwest through Sikkim. At the halfway point they trespassed onto forbidden Nepalese ground after crossing over Jonsong La. The team had hired a small contingent of Gurkhas to protect them from Tibetan brigands, but their luck held and they had no untoward encounters. They were, however, detained for a couple days in Ghunsa by a Nepalese official from Kathmandu. They sweet-talked their way out of a possible and potentially embarrassing diplomatic faux pas, and continued on over Kang La back into Sikkim.

It had never been our intention to follow in the exact footsteps of Freshfield and Sella. (Border politics between Nepal, India and Tibet, also made it impossible.) Their adventure merely inspired ours. Nor did our trek resemble anything of a circle around Kangchenjunga. As Pat noted, "it's looking more like a pretzel than a circle." Part of that pretzel touched Kathmandu.

After two days of permit wrangling and food buying, we were ready for what Freshfield called a "formidable adventure" in the eastern Himalaya. We had two options: a nerve rattling, three-day bus ride followed by another day of hiking to our trail head in Taplejung; or two quick flights.

A bus trip on the back roads of Nepal is like entering a lunatic asylum on wheels. A manic driver – and they are all manic – begins by revving his engine and then slipping the clutch so the whole assembly lurches forward whether passengers are on or off. Once underway, the shrill, overamplified songs of popular Hindi films pierce the eardrums. Nearly every Nepali man, woman and child is addicted to tobacco, so the squalid interior soon fills with acrid cigarette smoke. Chickens, bags of cement, potatoes and produce somehow fill up the limited space remaining once you have filled the narrow seats with your own frame. The smell of unwashed feet and armpits gives the whole experience an earthy olfactory quality. After six or seven hours of such mental and physical torture, a traveler comes to the mid-point of the journey, only to realize there is still another six hours to come.

Having tasted the dubious pleasures of Asian bus travel one too many times, the decision for Pat and me was obvious. We would fly. How could we go wrong stepping aboard a carrier with a name like Cosmic Air, Yeti Airways or Buddha Air?

Four of us would fly to Biratnagar, Nepal's second largest city, on the far southeastern border with India. Dave and Davin, both in their mid-20s and ever keen to throw themselves headlong into new experiences, would join our friend Lhakpa Tsering Sherpa, sirdar Lal Bahadur and porters for the three day bus ride to the trail head.

From the air Nepal's foothills look like one of the planet's most over-used landscapes. Almost half of the country's 21 million people – 90 percent of whom are subsistence farmers – live in its mountains. Prime real estate in the narrow valley bottoms went years ago. As a consequence, Nepalis have settled the steep hillsides and carved them into terraced fields that resemble huge staircases. To make way for agriculture – and to feed the hungry mouths of their many children – the farmers have cut down much of Nepal's forests.

My attention was drawn to the horizon in the north where a cluster of snowy peaks appeared. I immediately recognized the rock pyramid of Everest. It peered haughtily above the rampart of Lhotse, a mountain nearly as high and in reality considerably more difficult to climb than its celebrated neighbor. Slightly to the east stood another 8000-meter peak, Makalu. Much further to the east, separate and aloof from the others, was Kangchenjunga. This snowy landmark shores up the eastern end of a row of 8000-meter-high titans. Nepal has eight of the world's fourteen 8000-meter mountains within its borders. And on this one short flight we could see half of them.

We touched down in Biratnagar and then flew northward the next morning. Kangchenjunga loomed on the horizon like a shining beacon. Through the cockpit window I scanned the sea of sharp ridges ahead of us, trying to pick out our route. From the west side of the mountain spilled the Tamur River. We planned to walk from Taplejung northward up its drainage system to Kangchenjunga's north base camp at Pangpema (spitting distance from Nepal Gap, our high point of the previous spring). From there our trail backtracked a little and then rounded the southwest corner of the massif along a series of high passes where Jannu stands like a wary sentinel. Dubbed by early climbers the "Peak of Terror," its beautiful, sphinx-shaped profile reinforces its threatening nickname.

After visiting Kangchenjunga's south base camp up the Yalung Valley, our team would descend to the lowlands. Only Pat, Margie and I would cross the Indian border by road at Kakarbitta to revisit Darjeeling and Gangtok. The finishing touch would be a trek into the Dzongri area to Goecha La, the pass looking into the south face of Kangchenjunga. That is where Freshfield reached his final high point before he returned to Darjeeling. All in all this journey would consume almost two months.

The landing strip above Taplejung resembled an inclined cricket field that had been carved out of a ridge top with primitive hand-held tools. I tightened my seat belt as we bumped to a noisy, grinding halt. The plane door sprang open and cool, fresh mountain air surged in. I took a deep breathe and a familiar feeling inside of me stirred – I felt at home.

In 1987 Pat and I had visited Taplejung at the end of an ambitious seven-month journey. It was another grand circle idea, but this one encompassed the whole Himalayan range. With two American friends we traveled from Lhasa across Tibet into western China, and then down the Karakorum Highway from Kashgar into Pakistan. After crossing northern India we ended up in Nepal. Our transport included mountain bikes, trucks, buses, trains and donkey carts; we were in no rush.

We had wanted to complete the circle by returning to Lhasa. But the suppression of pro-independence riots by Chinese soldiers that year forced us to abandon those plans. As a finale we trekked into the Makalu area to the west of Taplejung. We had also wanted to seek out Kangchenjunga, then off-limits to foreigners. The police predictably refused to extend our visas and trekking permits. Now we were keen to pick up the trail abandoned some 11 years earlier.

From the postage-stamp-size airstrip we walked slowly down the steep trail to Taplejung behind a Tibetan horseman and his gray steed carrying our duffel bags. After an hour we entered main street, a narrow, cobblestone lane only slightly wider than a hiking trail. It curved around the hillside, revealing a bustling ribbon of commerce. It was Saturday – market day – and villagers from outlying areas had come into town. The many open-fronted shops plied aluminum pots, spicy samosas, clocks, striped polyester sweat pants, rubber boots, dried fish, Khukuri Rum, colorful yarn and pineapple-cream biscuits – the necessities of life. The dead eyes of a freshly butchered water buffalo stared dolefully from the street-side chopping block as a cluster of villagers bargained over its haunches.

We found the Namge Hotel, a rustic but clean trekker's lodge, on a side lane. Namge, the owner, was off in Kathmandu with his two sons. But his very capable wife, Dawa Bhote, whom we addressed with the honorific title, Ama-la, kept the place running with the efficiency of a hardened Tibetan trader. The family's origins were no secret. The walls of the hotel's restaurant proudly displayed pictures of the Dalai Lama and the Potala Palace, the Maitreya Buddha (the Buddha of the Future), a thangka and the requisite mug shot of the King of Nepal and his family.

The newly built stone hotel had five small rooms on the second floor; their walls were covered with whitewashed mud while the floors were made of rough-planked wood. A rickety bed with a straw-stuffed mattress offered Pat, still recovering from a bronchial infection that he picked up in Kathmandu, a suitable place to rest.

I went out to wander. Taplejung still seemed like a timeless mountain village. Women sat on low stools in the sunshine, chatting to each other and casually picking lice from their children's hair. Teen-aged boys crowded around boards set up on barrels where they flicked checker-sized discs into corner pockets in a popular game called *karem*. Scarlet-combed roosters crowed with hoarse bravado even though the sun had risen hours ago.

But electricity and bulldozers were inching closer towards the district headquarters along the muddy ruts of a new road. Engineered by Koreans and designed to initially connect local tea estates in the foothills, the 220-kilometer-long road extends northward from the East-West Highway that joins Kathmandu with India. Villagers told me that the final few kilometers to Taplejung would be completed in 1999. The shock troops of modernity – TVs, satellite dishes and public telephone and fax services – had already arrived. Soon noisy, diesel-belching buses and trucks would spew noxious fumes into the bucolic village.

I stepped into a shop for a cup of *chiya*, the sweet milk tea that is popular in Nepal. A friendly young Sherpa stood in the doorway. Dressed in jeans, a baseball cap and cowboy boots, he would easily blend in at the popular Calgary bar called Cowboys. He was on his way to Kathmandu to study business management.

"Is this your first time to Nepal?" he asked in excellent English.

"Ah, no," I answered. "This is my fifth time. I must like Nepal a lot."

He laughed as he gestured toward the big peaks to the north. "We live here, but we don't go anywhere," he teased. Then the Sherpa grew serious. "Nepal is a very poor country, you know. It is not good."

I had heard this line many times from Nepalis. World Bank statistics rate Nepal as one of the 25 least-developed nations on this planet. Grants and foreign aid loans make up half of the country's budget. But by trying to improve the standard of living, world aid has inadvertently convinced Nepalis that they are so poor that they cannot succeed without it. Hand-outs of any magnitude – from trail-side candy to hydroelectric dams – have turned Nepalis into recreational beggars and corporate panhandlers.

"But if Nepal is not good," I argued, "why do you think so many foreigners come here?" The Sherpa shrugged, kicking at a pebble with his shiny pointy-toed boot, and then laughed. He had no answer.

Our motivation for coming was simple: to walk and live among some the world's most gracious and friendly people. Freshfield was motivated by similar pleasures and a strong sense of mountain worship. "I have always traveled and climbed for scenery first, for science afterwards, and – let me add – for all that is included under the modern term 'records' last." We could not put it any clearer than that.

But many trekkers often overlook the simple joys that life on the trail can offer. Of Nepal's 300,000 annual visitors, roughly a quarter of that number come to walk in the mountains. Many genuinely want to learn about the people and customs of the Himalaya. But others are simply drawn to Nepal because it is a cheap way-station on the vagabond circuit of southeast Asia.

At the Namge Hotel we met two sullen Austrians whose faces had been reddened by wind and sun. That evening we tried to coax some conversation from the pair as they hunched over bowls of noodle soup at the next table.

"How was your trek?" I asked, anxious to hear of the trail ahead.

"Oh, zer were too many groups," they replied tersely. We looked at each other, puzzled by their ingratitude.

"Maybe next time you should go to northern Canada," Margie suggested. "You're guaranteed not to see any other people – only mosquitoes, muskrats and polar bears up there." The two found little humor in her comment and soon retreated to their room.

Their reaction reminded me of what our good friend and certified "Nepal-a-holic," Stephen Bezruchka, has observed. "Some trekkers complain that Nepal isn't all it was billed to be," he noted. "And then they search for new unspoiled places to desecrate." As the author of the guidebook, *Trekking in Nepal*, Stephen was certainly as guilty of popularizing Nepal among *bedeshis,* or foreigners, as Pat and I were with our articles and photographs. But the danger of erasing what is worth discovering comes with each and every journey. We hoped, at least, that our footprints had been gentle and respectful ones.

While waiting for the rest of our bus-bound party we became reacquainted with the simple joys of *thomba*. The mildly potent grog of fermented millet seeds served with hot water and sipped through a bamboo straw is a special drink of the Limbus – a kind of Himalayan gluhwein. (Freshfield noted that "taken at rare intervals and in small doses it is, in default of anything better, refreshing.") At the hotel, Ama-la served thombas in tall, hardwood vessels decorated with brass rings. She was an expert thomba maker. Pat, luckily, was now back in drinking form, and Margie and Ilana quickly became devotees.

On the third afternoon Dave and Davin, looking rather dusty and tired from walking in the lowland heat, arrived with our entourage of porters and AmaDablam staff. Davin drew long thirsty gulps from a Star beer while Dave described their bus adventure. "What a trip! Kerosene started leaking from the plastic containers at the back of the bus and was soon slopping all over the floor. The fumes got so nauseating that we sat on the roof for the rest of the way. Up on top, it always felt like the bus was going to tip over like a top-heavy boat. You know how it is going around countless switchbacks. But one of the porters kept assuring us, 'Slipping, not tipping.'"

"Well, you can be thankful you missed out on the true Nepal experience of slipping *and* tipping," replied Pat.

With our ranks reunited, we were almost ready to hit the trail. Our gear included 200 litres of kerosene (minus whatever had leaked out), 80 kilograms of rice, some 370 eggs and a folding table and chairs. It lay piled in the yard like a mini-Kangchenjunga. Our porters, a rag tag group from a mixture of hill tribes – Magar, Tamang, Limbu and Rai – secretly assessed their chances of getting a less desirable load, like a smelly kerosene container, or a delicate one such as egg cartons piled one top of the other. Most of our 25 porters had been hired in Kathmandu, since it is difficult to find locals in the foothills willing to abandon their fields during harvest time.

Portering remains the backbone of Nepal's transportation infrastructure. In a land with few roads, and trails often too steep for pack animals, human porters are the "truck drivers" of the Himalaya. From river bottoms to high mountain passes they will carry just about anything, including awkward loads of corrugated tin for roofing, conduit pipe and huge bales of wire – all with a tump line called a *namlo*. Their compact, sinewy bodies strain under loads that sometimes exceed their own body weight. Our porters were expected to carry a load of 30 kilograms. You could easily spot the professionals because they carried *a teko*. The carved, T-shaped stick provides balance on slippery slopes and serves as a support for resting loads.

Most foreign trekkers learn to appreciate the physical and moral strength of the Nepali people from their porters. But due to language barriers, it is difficult to get to know them as well as the trekking agency staff. The sirdar, guide and cook are often conversant in several languages.

The man in charge of our porters was 34-year-old Lal Bahadur, nicknamed Lale (pronounced Laleh). As an old hand in the trekking business, this sirdar had worked his way up from carrying heavy loads to managing trekking groups. He had the tough look of a foreman – a mop of short-cropped raven-black hair and an imitation leather jacket, black jeans and a black baseball cap worn like a barrio gang leader. Lale was a Magar, from a hill tribe well known for its honesty and work ethic. Both the Magar and Gurung men, proud of their fighting abilities, are often named Bahadur, meaning brave. I wondered if there was a story of bravado behind the small scar on the left side of Lale's face, but none was forthcoming. During our month-long trek we counted on his good humor and fast smile to keep the porters in check.

Every trekking crew has its pecking order. After the sirdar came the cook. Dil, a Newari from the Kathmandu Valley, was Lale's brother in law. With the help of a few faithful underlings Dil could create an endless repertoire of delicacies on a couple of temperamental single-burner kerosene stoves. Each evening he would enter the dining tent, flip his baseball cap around to the back of his head with a flourish and serve up the first of several dishes as we oohed and aahed like kids watching Houdini pull a rabbit out of a hat. Even with an icy wind ripping at the tent door, he produced culinary delights like pizza, cake and what he called a pumpkin pie – a whole steamed pumpkin crammed with a sweet cinnamon stuffing. (Pat – who has the appetite of a Yukon sled dog – has always maintained, "Happy stomachs make happy campers.") As we gained altitude our appetites predictably waned and we requested simpler fare, like boiled potatoes and the Nepali staple of *dal bhaat* (lentils and rice), which is both nutritious and easy to digest.

The AmaDablam guide, 24-year-old Manish Suba, also held stature within our group. This was his first time guiding, and he had come along to learn the route. His fledgling status earned him the nickname "Nepali tourist." With perfectly groomed hair and a bandana sewn to his cap, Lawrence-of-Arabia-style, he bounded up the trail with long strides. The battered 35 mm camera hanging around his neck added the definitive touch. As a Limbu his ancestors hailed from the Taplejung area, although he was now a city boy studying in Kathmandu. He was full of enthusiasm, not only for his new job, but also for life lived in a modern world.

But of all the unique personalities in our crew, Lhakpa Tsering Sherpa was clearly the star. Pat first got to know him as one of his two Everest summit partners in 1982 on the first Canadian expedition. Since then Lhakpa has been to Everest many more times, including three other successful summit bids. The Sherpa was also on the mountain in May of 1996 when the famous New Zealand guide Rob Hall perished along with his client at 8700 meters after reaching the top. In his account of the tragedy Jon Krakauer wrote of Lhakpa's unsuccessful attempt to rescue Hall. (Unfortunately Krakauer misspelled the name as Lhakpa Chhiri Sherpa.)

Although Lhakpa did not work for AmaDablam, we had invited him along on this trip to be Pat's camera assistant. In addition to carrying photographic equipment,

A woman from the Limbu hill tribe, a warrior caste of eastern Nepal,
greets us on the trail up to the high country.

he could also help break the ice when we wanted to get portraits of locals. He was used to working as a sirdar for trekking groups, and now, even though his responsibilities were minimal, he was always on the look-out for something to do. He often helped the AmaDablam crew with chores such as setting up the tents or just encouraged the porters when things got tough.

"Dzum," Lhakpa, an ever-cheerful Buddhist, now said. "Let's go." His smiling spirit was so strong that it could melt a mountain glacier. Ushered along by Lhakpa's singing, we traipsed down the trail.

Quintessential Nepal now revealed itself to us. Golden terraced fields of millet swayed in the breeze as farmers sliced off the ripe heads of grain with sickle-shaped *dashi* knives. In spite of our foreignness, people opened their doors and welcomed us. No traveler in Nepal need ever feel lonely.

As we descended to the Tamur River the air grew hot and sticky, even though the monsoon had quit a month ago. This wetter, eastern region is well known for its leeches. These heat-seeking bloodsuckers surreptitiously infiltrate socks and pant legs through the tiniest holes. Once, one of our porters detected a leech inexplicably stuck to the roof of his mouth. But at this time of year the onset of winter concerned us more than bloodsuckers.

Several of the trekkers that we met coming down from the high country warned of sub-zero nighttime temperatures. "Ah, we're Canadians. We can handle the cold," we boasted. But I worried about the porters. The agency had issued them with extra clothing like lined nylon jackets and pants, but they would need more protection than that at the higher altitudes. They did not have insulated sleeping bags, for instance. We had brought along some extra hats, mitts and pile jackets from Canada and hoped that the additional clothing would suffice.

For now we enjoyed the heat of the foothills, where tree-sized poinsettias flaunted their scarlet bracts like rouge-cheeked ladies of the night. Here and there ivory-white blossoms of frangipani littered the ground. Their petals lay next to trail-side piles of cow dung and lesser, yet equally dangerous, mounds of human excrement, usually deposited by young children. At the outskirts of villages we walked vigilantly.

In the hamlet of Hangdewa we stopped at a *chautaara*, a ubiquitous trailside resting place for porters, usually in the shade of a big banyan tree. Manish, our Nepali tourist, immediately befriended 76-year-old Indra Bahadur, a fellow Limbu. As our

A porter crosses a dilapidated bridge repaired with bamboo poles near Chirwa.

A typical bridge from a century ago constructed entirely from bamboo poles. PHOTO: VITTORIO SELLA

young guide posed questions to him, the old Gurkha's milky eyes began to light up as he told war stories about fighting the Japanese in Siam, Burma and Indonesia.

In Nepal the Gurkhas are as famous as the Sherpas. *Gurkha* is a collective expression that applies to the Magars, Limbus, Gurungs and Rais who served in the British army. Ever since Nepal sent its Gurkha troops to aid the British Raj during the Indian mutiny in the 1850s, the British have valued their ferocity and courage. More than 30,000 Gurkhas fought in World Wars I and II with great distinction.

In a moment of sudden spryness that belied his age, Indra Bahadur dropped to his belly to show how he had crawled through the jungle to evade machine gun fire. People like this old Limbu made trekking in Nepal a special pleasure. You do not have to know much Nepali to *gauf garne* – to shoot the breeze. In places without cell phones and television the pleasantries of gossip have not been lost.

"Kahaa jaanei didi?" asked curious villagers. (Where are you going, big sister?) *"Kahaa baata aaeko?"* (Where are you coming from?) But in Nepal, distance is more of a concept than a well-defined measurement. To gauge the length of time it takes to travel between any two points the Nepalis use a *rumali mil* or "handkerchief mile." That's the amount of time it takes a wet hankie to dry while walking.

In the village of Sinwa, we stopped for some tea and oranges. A rambunctious Limbu woman, perhaps a little tipsy from one too many thombas, cajoled us. As we shook hands, Lhakpa did the translating. "She is asking if Ilana is your daughter." I was taken aback at this inference. If I had been a Nepali, of course, I should have had lots of children and grandchildren by the age of 43. I shook my head and laughed. She then grabbed Ilana's arm and pulled her closer.

"She is asking if Ilana wants to be her daughter-in-law," Lhakpa laughed. "She has a nice son who is 18 years old." At that Ilana recoiled good naturedly, and we bade our farewell before any further matchmaking could take place.

On our first day we walked little more than three hours. Dave was grateful for that. Usually bursting with energy and enthusiasm, he now lay incapacitated by a stomach bug in a sore heap in the shade. We unhurriedly set up camp in a farmer's fallow field at Mitlung. Time filled the day like a hot air balloon drifting across the clear sky. A baby tarantula waddled into the grass.

Having dumped their loads, our porters pulled out a pack of cards and sat in a cluster on the ground. In fact, whenever we stopped, the cards came out and the guys got involved in an animated game. They played seriously, slapping the cards down on the grass with exaggerated emphasis. Lhakpa matched his wits with Lale and the boys, earning portions of their hard-earned wages as well as their respect.

Lhakpa was very much a fun-loving party animal. He was always the first to toss in the ante during a betting game, and he loved his *rakshi,* Nepali fire water. I knew I could count on him as my thomba partner. In fact, I knew I could count on him, no matter what we were doing. Lhakpa was a friend. He and his cousin Ang Nima came to Canada in 1992 as guests of the Canadian team to Everest. For part of his three-month visit, the two Sherpas stayed with us and another climber friend in Canmore. Lhakpa had good memories of that trip.

"Hey, Lhakpa. Do you remember wing night at the Drake pub?" Pat asked him after the card game had finished.

"Oh, yeah. Every Wednesday night. Good and spicy," he replied, smacking his lips.

"What do you remember best from Canada, Lhakpa?" questioned Davin.

"Paragliding from Mount Lady MacDonald," shot back the Sherpa. The memory of soaring tandem 1000 meters above Canmore and the Bow Valley – like a carefree *garuda,* a mythical half-man, half-bird – lit up his rugged face. During his visit he heliskied for a day in the Cariboo mountains, rollerbladed in Vancouver's Stanley Park, saw the ocean for the first time and became an honorary Canadian by watching *Hockey Night in Canada* with the requisite beer in hand. I often wondered what he really thought about it all. But in typical non-judgmental fashion, he would only laugh and shrug. For Lhapka things were *not* better or worse than something else; they just were as they were.

Our Sherpa friend had traveled far in this world with just six years of education. He had learned to read and write Nepali in a dirt-floored schoolroom and later taught himself how to read and write English. He sported an expensive watch from Japan and new Swiss boots. Life was beautiful.

I slept well that night, lulled to sleep by droning cicadas. The murmur of the nearby river added to the peace. Each morning we hit the trail after 7 A.M. The porters had their own routine. Before we had even eaten breakfast, they were on their way. They typically walked a few hours before having the first of two daily meals. To cook up a pot of dal bhaat they would find a tea house or friendly hearth in someone's home.

As we ascended the Tamur Valley, the gorge became narrower and the mountains threatened to swallow us. Our group was adapting well to life on the trail. Although Ilana's stiff new leather hiking boots were giving her blisters, she maintained an unhurried pace in her long green skirt. I had advised both Ilana and Margie to wear skirts while hiking along the trail. The skimpy shorts and tank tops worn by so many Western trekkers offend local sensibilities. Shorts on men is fine – in the Hindu caste system it simply places the wearer at the lowest rung on the social ladder.

Big Dave, a friendly giant in mismatched socks, now had his rebellious stomach under control and strode up the trail easily. Davin, the well-honed athlete, charged ahead. He would sit and read one of his many books while waiting for us to catch up. His bulging thighs and mop of bushy blonde hair turned many a Nepali head.

Margie found joy in the gentle pace of walking and the novelty of being "the client." After 20 years of looking after lodge guests, she now enjoyed being taken care of. "I've never done something like this before where I'm the one who just sits back and lets someone else do all the work, carry my stuff, cook for me, take care of me like this. Is this what you call a holiday?" confessed our friend.

Pat and I slipped into the routine with equal ease. Darkness and the lack of electricity made it easy to go to bed early each night (8:30 P.M. would constitute a late night). In the mornings, at first light, we waited for quiet footsteps and a cheery voice to announce, "Good morning, *didi*. Good morning, *dai*. Bed tea." We then unzipped the tent door and gratefully accepted a steaming mug of sweet *chiya*. I brushed and braided my hair and we packed the duffel bags. We ate breakfast and started walking. It was a simple and fulfilling routine.

On the third day we reached the Ghunsa Valley, a narrow defile branching off to the northeast. Further up the Tamur lay the ancient trading village of Walungchung Gola, close to the Tibetan border. The village was a two-day walk away and off-limits to us. Yet the notion of taking a detour from our intended route and visiting its ancient monastery appealed to me. We decided to stop at the hamlet of Lelep, high above the junction of the Ghunsa River with the Tamur, where the Kangchenjunga Conservation Area Project office was located.

"Let's just see if we can wangle a permit," I suggested.

Lelep was a pretty Sherpa village of some 20 houses, perched high on the steep hillside with a gunshot view of Jannu. We found the Conservation office and its four staff members in a small sunny courtyard. They seemed surprised to see us. One pulled out brand new folding chairs still partially wrapped in plastic. Another ordered an underling to bring tea.

When the Nepali government opened this remote and rugged area to trekking in 1988, very few groups came. But now nearly a decade later the Ministry of Tourism estimates 10,000 visitors come every year. Still, this is not many compared to the Everest and Annapurna regions, which attracted 18,000 and 51,000 respectively in 1999. The office had the difficult job of monitoring trekkers, teaching villagers about community values and keeping an eye on the environment. In this isolated, quiet village, I speculated that they would also be playing a lot of cards.

"Are we your first visitors?" I asked.

"Yes, you are," replied one conservation officer matter-of-factly. "It is a new office, only nine months old, and besides, foreigners are not supposed to come here." These officials obviously were not about to give us a permit. Their coolness towards us lessened somewhat when I pulled out a postcard of Canmore and described how our home town of 10,000 people sat on the edge of a national park. Not wanting to ruin their day we omitted any mention of the subdivisions and golf courses now displacing the valley's wildlife.

After thanking the officials for tea, we walked up to the Lelep gompa. Lama Tenzing, reeking of mid-afternoon thomba, pulled out the key and let us in. The monastery was sadly run down. Most of its precious relics had been stolen. All that remained inside were a few broken statues. Even the sacred Kanjur books lay in their cubby holes, rotting and dejected. Faith can come and go with the seasons in the Himalaya.

Outside the gompa a group of curious women and kids gathered around us. Davin pulled out some photographs of his family and friends. He kept the pictures protected in a Ziploc bag. Curiously, the villagers paid little attention to the people. They were more interested in the three family dogs, two of which looked like Lhasa apsos, a Pekingese-type dog proudly kept in many Tibetan monasteries and families.

As we headed up the Ghunsa Valley, we found fewer villages and people. I stopped at a hut made of thin wood planks. A poor farmer wearing cut-off rubber boots and a dirty rag wrapped around his head, turban-style, motioned to me to enter. In Nepal a stranger can stick his or her head into anyone's house and be welcomed. Locked doors do not exist. Around a fire fueled by dried corn cobs sat another traveler. He was a Sherpa with a load of cheroots, local cigarettes, returning to his family's home and shop in Ghunsa. He poured some roasted soybeans out of a plastic bag into my palm. I repaid this kind gesture with a smile.

We made camp at a beautiful place called Gyalpa, a flat meadow hanging high above the Ghunsa River. Lunch was waiting for us all laid out on a maroon table cloth. Umbahadur stood ready with cups of hot lemon drink. We were hungry and devoured coleslaw (made safe by soaking the raw cabbage in a solution of potassium permanganate), french fried potatoes, curried vegetables and pancakes.

I leaned back and smiled at Margie, the tough mountain guide.

"OK," said Margie. "So I'm not embarrassed about the chairs now. Nor the table, nor the porters carrying my stuff," she added contentedly. We all felt a little self-conscious about the trailside catering. Back at home we carried our own loads and prepared our meals. But the colonials had created a certain standard of travel and service in the Himalaya, and we decided not to resist it. Meanwhile our crew brought out a volleyball and started a boisterous circle game.

A group of elderly British trekkers suddenly appeared on the trail stabbing the ground with basketless ski poles. "Can you tell me, please," one woman asked. "Is this some kind of youth camp for Nepali kids? They were playing soccer up there," as she pointed to where a French group was camped higher up. "And now here are others playing volleyball."

We tried to keep a straight face. "Well, ma'am, they are our porters and I guess they just have too much energy," replied Davin. "Maybe we should give them heavier loads tomorrow so they're more tired at the end of the day."

We camped next at Amjilassa, a small settlement that consisted of half a dozen Sherpa houses clinging to the gorge. We pitched our tents on a narrow terrace above the first house we saw. The undertones of constant chanting came from inside the house. The family had commissioned a monk from Ghunsa's gompa to conduct prayers for good health, an act that would benefit all others in the village, including the bedeshis.

After supper, our porters clustered around the warmth and sustenance of flame in the tiny yard. A few of us went inside the house to visit the monk. The meter-wide, hand-hewn floorboards, now well worn with age, testified to the size of the trees that once grew in Nepal's forests. Two posters on the wall flaunted handsome

Nepali youth in jeans. Lit by a solitary oil lamp these modern images looked out of place next to a monk sitting cross-legged by the window. Lama Lobsang was already sipping on a thomba in the wavering darkness.

Manish and Lhakpa translated as we asked the monk about Kangchenjunga. We wondered if Nepalis revered the mountain as much as their Sikkimese neighbours. Lama Lobsang readily explained that he and the other monks give pujas to the god of the mountain four times a year. They pray for protection from sickness, crop failure and landslides. The latter were big concerns. Our trail had traversed massive gouges where violent rock slides had ripped away the skin of mountainside. We crossed those sections with care, fully aware that airborne rocks could come whizzing down like missiles.

In the morning I awakened to Lama Lobsang's tranquil prayers. Our tent, positioned on the terrace two meters from the house, faced its tiny window. Now, as our bed tea arrived, Lama Lobsang stuck his head out and saluted us with his own cup of solja. His toothless smile beamed good karma into the morning air.

An old mastiff, tired from a night of barking at imaginary assailants, skulked around our camp. His right eye was crusted with puss and his snout dirty from scavenging our latrine under the cover of night. He looked on sadly as we ate porridge and eggs until Umbahadur shooed him off.

Every day we climbed upwards. Hidden peaks came into sight and then vanished. The weather took on a cold edge. Dave and Davin abandoned their shorts for long pants and I started wearing longjohns under my skirt. Hats and gloves stayed at the ready in the top of my pack. We entered a forest of huge fir, hemlock and larch. The yellowed needles of the larches tinkled to the ground as the days of autumn hastened into winter.

A hardy mixture of Sherpas and Tibetans live in this upper valley along with their yaks, the ubiquitous high-altitude beast of burden that provide meat, wool, leather, milk, butter and dung for fuel. Ilana shrieked with delight when she saw her first shaggy-haired creature. It was really a *dzopkio,* a yak/cow crossbreed, but that did not matter. With their long bushy tails and ears adorned with tufts of red wool these animals looked, as a friend once observed, like 'cows dressed up for the opera.'

Before the main village of Ghunsa we passed through Phole, a small Tibetan refugee settlement. Young rosy-cheeked women smiled and encouraged us to buy their turquoise, carpets and yak wool toques. Colorful skeins of newly dyed wool hung draped over the fences. Tibetans founded the village in 1959 after fleeing the Chinese takeover; to this day refugees continue to trickle across the border in search of a life free of persecution.

We visited the Tashi Chombe Gompa, one of two monasteries in Phole. Several enterprising locals had draped carpets and hats on the fence to encourage hesitant buyers. Tibetans built the gompa nearly 30 years ago, and it houses one of four Buddha statues dating back to the eighth century. The other three are in Lhasa, Beijing and Dharamsala, the headquarters of the Dalai Lama's government-in-exile.

Beyond Phole, we exited a sweet-scented fir and juniper forest and crossed the river to the village of Ghunsa. This warren of 50 weather-beaten houses seemed forlorn and its potato fields were gray and sandy. Unlike the solid stone Sherpa houses in Lhakpa's village of Kunde, none of these houses seemed to offer adequate protection against the elements. A snot-nosed village welcoming committee of children shouted "Namaste, give me one pen" from unseen corners.

Pursued by a dark, clammy fog we hastily set up camp in the yard of the Shree Selela Lodge, one of Ghunsa's four new lodges. Our orange tents flickered like oriental lanterns in the dullness. I looked forward to the prospect of staying more than one day in order to adjust to the altitude, now 3444 meters.

We went to visit a Sherpa woman we had met on the trail a few days before. "We drink thomba, have party," she promised. We now followed directions given to Lhakpa and found the house with blue-painted window sills at the upper edge of the village. She greeted us warmly. I called her didi and she called me didi.

"Basnos didi," my big sister said. "Sit down." I settled on a side bench covered with worn carpets. As expected, her kitchen was smoky and dark. Several blue plastic barrels lined the cluttered corners. The big containers, in addition to the Goretex, fleece and down clothing worn by a few of the villagers, were remnants of bygone expeditions.

Didi fussed over our thombas. She did not have enough bamboo straws to go around, so Pat ended up with one made from an old aluminum tent pole, which severely compromised the taste experience. Lhakpa taught me how to clean the straw to avoid catching any unwanted illness from previous imbibers. This required covering the hole of the straw with my thumb and then pumping it several times. The quick thumb action created a vacuum that sucked up the hot liquid. When I inverted the straw and released my thumb at the same time, the liquid flushed out any lingering microbes onto the dirt floor. Didi's batch, made of barley instead of the normal millet, tasted very good but was stronger than we thought, especially taken after a hard day of hiking.

Didi's husband, Tharkey, soon joined the party. He had sparkling eyes and spoke a little English. With Lhakpa acting as translator we chatted. Tharkey had six children and was wealthy enough to send his two oldest boys to boarding school in Darjeeling. The other kids still lived at home. His 15-year-old daughter tended the fire, poured water into our thombas and prepared supper. I asked her in Nepali if she went to school. She turned her head shyly to one side. Her younger brother interjected with an emphatic "No."

"You have baby?" asked Didi. I shook my head and answered, "*Chhoro-chori chhaina.*" (I don't have kids.) She laughed in disbelief. She probably thought something was drastically wrong with me. How could I explain to her that Pat and I were "conscientious objectors" who felt the world already had far too many people. Now, I watched her daughter locked in ignorance because she could not read or write, just

Ghunsa is a small village at 3444 meters inhabited by Sherpas and Tibetan refugees. Locals have built a few new guesthouses to accommodate the current annual influx of 10,000 trekkers to the region.

like her mother. We later saw Didi and several other women with children tied to their backs going to a literacy class. I hoped her daughter would be allowed to attend.

The pot on the fire bubbled, and soon Didi passed us a plate heaped with tiny boiled potatoes. I peeled one, dipped it into a mixture of chilis and salt and popped the hot morsel in my mouth. Potatoes have rarely tasted so good. With a mischievous wink Lhakpa agreed that they were, "almost as good as Khumbu potatoes."

Tharkey explained that every August he went on a trading trip to Tibet as his ancestors did. The nearest settlement, named Ruu, is one week's walk away. Throughout Nepal's borderlands, where food production rarely matches demand, the locals still rely on trans-Himalayan commerce. For trading in Tibet Tharkey usually brought along *churpi* (hard, dried cheese), butter, second-hand clothes, rice, and baby yaks (a one-year-old baby dzopkio is worth about US$180). He could exchange these goods for tea, shoes and wool. Sometimes he also brought back luxury items such as beer, coke and Wu Jiang cigarettes to sell to trekkers. And like many men, he also made another long journey to Kathmandu in the winter. There he found floor space with relatives, and tried to sell his wife's weavings.

Being an incurable trader, Tharkey soon asked if we wanted to buy anything. "You want carpet? Or maybe yak hair blankets, or this?" He held up a black saddle bag woven from the hairs of a yak tail.

"What about sheep bells?" asked Margie.

"Oh sorry, I don't have," said Tharkey. Not wanting to turn away a potential customer, he promised, "I will find for you."

Margie explained that she owned 12 sheep, a number that greatly impressed our host. "Oh, twelve sheeps?" he said. But his eyes turned round as his thomba mug when she said her brother owned 350 cattle. At this revelation, Tharkey whistled in amazement. In Nepal a herd of 50 yaks was considered enormous. Margie tried to explain Canadian ranches, but the numbers all seemed impossibly great.

With thomba buzzing through our blood and darkness obscuring the muddy trail back to our camp, we bade the family farewell and promised on our return to come back for the sheep bells. That night we feasted on Dil's heavenly goat curry that had us licking our chops. "Dil, the spices are all singing together," crooned Dave. Dil flashed a winning smile and his dreamy, movie star eyes shone in appreciation. The next night he used the rest of the meat to make momos, steamed, dough-wrapped dumplings that are the Himalayan snack equivalent of chicken wings.

I fell asleep that night listening to the sounds of the village. Drums echoed from a nearby lodge where porters sang and pounded out traditional rhythms. A dog barked madly. The voices of our porters, engaged in a marathon card game, carried musically through the night. Finally the gentle clanging of yak bells lulled me into dreams.

From Ghunsa onward we rested more in order to acclimatize properly. With each step up the valley we gained altitude. The land changed. Giant conifers now gave way to dwarfed trees and junipers the size of blueberry bushes. But as the vegetation grew smaller, the mountains loomed larger.

At Kambachen, a four-hour walk from Ghunsa, we took another so-called rest day. We brought out Freshfield's book and looked up Sella's picture of the village. The cluster of low stone houses backed against the hillside had changed little from a hundred years ago. Prayer flags on the ridgetop still fluttered in the stiff alpine breeze, just as Freshfield had seen them.

The mountain arena proved too alluring for sitting around. We crossed the Ghunsa

Ilana Cameron, Baiba and Margie Jamieson sample thomba, a popular drink brewed from fermented millet, at a tea shop along the way.

River to the west side and wandered up the alley of the glacial moraine toward the abrupt north face of Jannu. We stood, dazzled by the austere beauty, under the solid rampart of granite, ice and snow formed by the three peaks: Khabur (6332 meters), Sobithongie (6669 meters) and finally Jannu (7710 meters). After the wind began whipping up clouds of glacial silt hundreds of meters into the air, we turned back.

Up the trail from Kambachen, the rubble-strewn Kangchenjunga Glacier crowded the valley with its wide tongue of ice. Only a narrow band of meadow grew on the west side of its moraine where yaks found some grass to graze. We stopped for lunch below Mera Peak, its icy mantle perched above rocky shoulders. Table and chairs awaited us in a protected alcove among the big boulders. More than a hundred choughs swooped through the sky as if auditioning for a Hitchcock sequel.

We stopped a group of trekkers coming down the valley and asked them about conditions at Pangpema, Kangchenjunga's base camp. One of the members reported nighttime temperatures of minus 18 degrees Celsius and the near-loss of one tent to gusty winds. We soon met others on their way down from Lhonak. An older Swiss couple, victims of altitude sickness, stumbled by us, barely coherent.

After crossing a rickety log bridge over the Chabuk River we came to five huts in a broad meadow called Lhonak. Kangchenjunga still lay hidden behind one of its towering satellites, Wedge Peak. Our "Nepali youth crew" had already ditched their loads and were in the midst of a vigorous volleyball game. I passively sat and watched. I tried to ease a vague headache brought on by dehydration by drinking more water. At 4785 meters, it was important to go slowly and drink lots.

Sir Joseph Hooker experienced similar hardships crossing these high mountain passes. He wrote that the rare air made him feel like he had "a pound of lead on each knee-cap, two pounds in the pit of the stomach and a hoop of iron around the head."

Our group soon began to feel the way Hooker did. Both Dave and Davin slowed down, their heads pounding. As a well-honed, competitive skier, Davin did not like the idea of being short of breath. "My muscles feel spry, but my breathing can't keep up. The first thing I noticed was when I took a drink, I could only take two or three gulps at a time," he said. "It'd be hard to do a lot of necking around here. You'd have to come up for air a lot," added the good-looking athlete.

"Lucky there's no one to kiss around here," replied Dave, puckering his lips and winking at his tent mate.

Margie and Ilana were also struggling and arrived in camp an hour behind the rest of us. "That was one of the hardest days in my life!" announced Margie as she tossed her ski poles on the ground in disgust and slumped into a chair. All our trek companions were breaking their personal altitude records every day.

The sun went down and the coming darkness amplified the cold. Stars pricked the sky with a million pinholes. Yaks mulled about, impervious to the drop in temperature. Their bells clanged like wind chimes as they nibbled the overgrazed meadow.

In the morning both Margie and Ilana wisely decided to stay put another day to acclimatize. Ilana had gone to bed without eating much and felt nauseous during the night. Margie awoke with a headache but said she was not feeling too poorly. We were not overly concerned and left them at Lhonak with Lale and Umbahadur. They planned a day trek to Pangpema the following day.

Our frisky friend Lhakpa also was not faring well. But it was not from the altitude. Last night he had gone to visit a neighboring camp where a friend served as sirdar for a French group. Copious amounts of *rakshi* had been consumed and Lhakpa had danced the night away with two French women.

Dave Quinn and Davin Macintosh climb up the lower slopes of Mt. Drohma. Nepal Gap, our high point from the previous spring, separates Nepal Peak on the left from Kangchenjunga on the far right.

"I am a little hung over," he sheepishly admitted. "But it was a good party." Nevertheless, he kept up a steady stride and soon outpaced us.

I dawdled at the rear and let my body dictate a lazy pace. Manish, a keen walker, prudently turned back halfway with symptoms of altitude sickness. Just a week ago a helicopter evacuated a stricken trekker from Kambachen. Such incidents happen frequently when trekking groups force their members, acclimatized or not, to stick to unrealistic schedules.

It took three hours of slow, gentle walking to reach Pangpema. As we ascended a lateral moraine, the bony north ridge of Kangchenjunga finally revealed itself. One peak after another had blocked any view of the mountain for the longest time. Now the snowy abode fully occupied our vision in all its glory.

As soon as our porters dumped our gear at Pangpema they quickly walked back to Lhonak to find shelter in one of several stone huts. The few who remained set up our tents against the grassy hillside for wind protection. In 1995 four members of a Japanese group plus one Nepali died at this camp when two meters of wet snow slid down on their tent. One of Lhakpa's friends helped dig the bodies out. That devastating November snowstorm hit all of Nepal and killed a total of 63 people, including 22 foreigners. We eyed the steep slope above us warily.

Pangpema was a wedge of meadow, not much bigger than a football field, overlooking the junction of the Kangchenjunga and the Jonsong Glaciers. It was also the end of the trail, the end of vegetation and the end of Nepal. Tibet was less than 20 kilometers to the north. Jonsong La, the pass that mountaineers Douglas Freshfield, Frank Smythe and Dorjee Lhatoo had all crossed during their expeditions, beckoned out of sight to the north. In spite of the high altitude of 6145 meters, salt traders from Sikkim and Nepal at one time used the pass frequently.

Wild and austere mountains closed in around us like walls of a fortress. To the east, Nepal Peak, Tent Peak and The Twins formed the border with Sikkim. In the high notch that separated those peaks Pat spied Nepal Gap, his high point from six months ago. I wondered if the khata that he had left tied to a boulder was still there or if the wind had torn it away into the oblivion of Himalayan sky. On this side of the Gap, the slopes steepened into a severe, near-vertical wall of rock and ice that required technical climbing. We sat contentedly and made a visual ascent.

Terraces of ice and snow teetered on the steep north face of Kangchenjunga just

across the glacier. The wind harried the main summit with relentless force. Freshfield had made a note of the danger: "The whole face of the mountain might be imagined to have been constructed by the Demon of Kangchenjunga for the express purpose of defense against human assault, so skillfully is each comparatively weak spot raked by the ice and rock batteries." Kangchenjunga's climbing record supports Freshfield's early observation. Since its first ascent in 1955, only 143 people have climbed the mighty mountain. In contrast, Everest has been scaled by 808 climbers during 1,032 ascents.

At base camp Lhakpa told us a story about his cousin, Ang Nima, who had a near-fatal encounter with the wild gods of Kangchenjunga. Ang Nima, a long-time friend of ours, had worked with Pat on two Everest expeditions. In 1988 Ang Nima served as a high-altitude porter for an international team that included the American Carlos Buhler and Austrian Peter Habeler, climbing on the north ridge. (Together with Reinhold Messner, Habeler had been the first to climb Everest without oxygen in 1978.)

After carrying gear to the expedition's high camp Ang Nima and another Sherpa, Dawa Nuru, descended to Camp 2 for the night. A storm hit a few hours later, and a dangerous amount of snow began to accumulate. Sensing great danger, the two put on their boots and clothes yet remained in their sleeping bags. In the middle of the night an avalanche pummeled the tent and sent its human cargo tumbling a hundred meters downslope. Other avalanches repeatedly hit the men as they staggered down the mountain in pitch blackness. Just when Ang Nima thought he was sure to die, a ray of light guided them to fixed ropes leading to Camp 1. In the end the two men dragged themselves to safety. "The mountain gods on Kangchenjunga saved Ang Nima's life," concluded Lhakpa.

As daylight started to fade, a herd of 11 blue sheep, including three large rams, grazed near our tent door. Upslope more sheep dotted the hills. Oblivious to the wild animals, Lhakpa, Dil and the others stayed in the big tent playing cards. When the hiss of our pressure cooker broke the silence, the sheep scurried off into the dusk to the safety of higher slopes.

At dawn Pat and I lay curled up inside our toasty warm sleeping bags, somewhat immovable. Then we heard the familiar crunching of footsteps on frosted ground. I looked outside: another perfect day. The smiling faces of Umbahadur and Sanu, a porter with an Aunt Jemima-style handkerchief wrapped around his head, greeted me.

Lhakpa and Margie cross the Nupchu Khola at Kambachen as the early morning sun warms the air.

"Kasto chha?" I asked the two kitchen helpers with the tea kettle. ("How are you?") *"Ramro chha,"* they answered, as they always did. They were always fine. I looked at Sanu's bare feet and flip-flops and wondered why he was not wearing shoes in this cold.

"Ali ali jaado?" I persisted. "You sure you're not cold?" He answered with a big grin. *"Jaado, taa chaina, didi."* The lads poured our tea and we soon climbed out of our bags. "Do you think Freshfield started his days in such a civilized manner?" I asked Pat.

"Of course. He and his colonial buddies wrote the rule book," he replied.

We lingered around camp in the gentle sun until nearly noon. To capture the rich late-afternoon light, Pat, Lhakpa, Dave and Davin climbed with their cameras to a 6000-meter-high spur of Drohma Peak. I felt content to stay put and write.

A little later, a breathless Lale marched up the trail with disconcerting news. Margie had fallen sick yesterday afternoon. We did not realize just how sick until a few days later. With the help of some porters including Manish she had made her way down first to Kambachen and then to Ghunsa. Ilana had started out with Lale that morning but had run out of energy and turned around. Our group was now spread out in three different places. Lale ate a quick lunch and returned down the trail to catch up with the ailing.

As the day's shadows lengthened, I ventured high up on the hill and found a promontory overlooking the glacier. On a hut-sized boulder I built a cairn with two round stones and a hardened tangerine I had carried for days from the foothills. I sat down, feeling joy and great privilege to be here. I thought of my brother Uldis, a keen climber and skier with a similar penchant for traveling. His body lies forever entombed in a serac collapse below the Grand Combin in the Swiss Alps. I thought, too, of Margie's garrulous late partner, Art. I knew their spirits still soared in the mountains, riding the wind with the choughs, lammergeiers and garudas.

Next morning, a pinkish haze covered the shoulders of Kangchenjunga, suggesting a change in weather. We pulled up camp and began our descent. By late afternoon, the skies had turned an ominous slate gray. But by then Pat, Lhakpa and I were sitting around the warmth of the fire at the very basic Kangchenjunga Hotel in Kambachen. We learned that Margie had stayed here before continuing to Ghunsa.

In the hotel's kitchen Dil was drinking something Lhakpa called "fried *chang*". "Want to try some?" asked our cook. Of course we did. Dil melted some butter, added

Mt. Jannu (7710 meters), is a familiar, if not daunting sight to villagers
who live high above Khabeli Khola Valley.

a spoonful of cooked rice and a raw egg. He then poured in some chang, the sake-like rice or barley beer of these highland areas. It was a perfect cold-weather drink.

It snowed overnight. We were happy to be far from Pangpema and Lhonak. At Ghunsa we anxiously looked for Margie and Ilana, but they had gone off for a day's hike to test their level of acclimatization. They showed up a few hours later, having made a 1000-meter climb and descent without any problems.

With teas in hand we later listened to Margie's dramatic tale. As we hiked to Pangpema, she got very ill at Lhonak. To alleviate her nausea and headache, she took a dose of acetazolamide. It did not help. By 4 P.M. her condition had worsened. She knew that she had to get down to a lower altitude at Ghunsa as quickly as possible – the only sure way to alleviate symptoms of high-altitude sickness. Together with Manish and Umbahadur and a few other porters Margie set out with about two hours of light left to spare. A hundred meters beyond Lhonak she asked the porters if they could find a yak to carry her.

As her senses failed, the others began to take turns carrying the tough mountain woman by piggy-back. "I felt like I was completely losing it" she recalled. "All I could do was hang on and hope for the best. There was a pink glow in the sky, and I really felt like this was it. I had to keep taking big deep breaths to get my act together." Darkness soon overtook the party. One by one their flashlights dimmed and failed. Now Margie's lone headlamp lit the way for her rescuers, until it too, died. The porters carefully picked their way through the winding, bouldered trail in the dark. By 10 P.M. they reached Kambachen, where Margie collapsed into a deep sleep. Next morning, she had recovered enough to hike down to Ghunsa on her own. There Ilana caught up with her the next day.

Pat kidded Margie about "using her spurs" on the porters during her emergency piggy-back descent. But altitude sickness can hit the strongest and savviest of climbers anytime. A Canadian doctor later told us that if Margie had ignored her symptoms, as less experienced hikers often do, she might have died.

The weather kept us pinned in Ghunsa. A gentle, gray rain hissed like falling grains of sand off our tents. Lhakpa proclaimed it a "sleep day." Every now and then the clouds lifted, revealing a low snow line which meant heavy accumulation on the mountains. Because we had three high passes ahead of us, we happily waited out the weather.

In the afternoon the rain ceased and a curious visitor appeared out of the gloom.

Accompanied by three porters, a neatly dressed Japanese man stopped at the lodge. Katsuyuki Ono was an artist and looked the part with his beard and wire-trimmed glasses. For the last 53 days he had painted alone in the mountains. We had spotted his mysterious blue tarp and tent high above the trail on Mt. Shaphu above Kambachen.

"May I see your paintings?" I asked boldly. He fussed around with his bags and finally said, "OK."

After days of isolation the artist now faced his first critics and knew it. Like a lama revealing a sacred relic, he carefully undid a bundle wrapped in plastic. He set down on the ground the canvases that were still drying. The others he unrolled slowly. Jannu and Kangchenjunga, the same mountains that we had photographed for the last 10 days, now lay before us in colorful acrylics.

"Have you heard of Nicholas Roerich?" I asked Katsuyuki. His face brightened. "Ah yes, famous Russian painter," said the Japanese man.

The colors in Katsuyuki's paintings strongly reminded me of Roerich, who lived from 1874 to 1947. He was smitten by his first view of Kangchenjunga while visiting Darjeeling in 1924. He often painted the grand massif in vibrant blues, pinks and purples. And he praised the Himalaya as being a singular "abode of light" where "the

This photograph of Jannu from near Sele La remains one of Vittorio Sella's most compelling mountain portraits.
PHOTO: VITTORIO SELLA

highest knowledge, the most inspired songs, the most superb sounds and colors are created."

Roerich, a stern-looking man with a completely bald head and a Lenin-style beard, was multi-talented. He produced some 7,000 paintings, 30 books and even painted the set and costume designs for the modern ballet productions of Nijinsky, Stravinsky and Diaghilev. He also established an international arts center called Corona Mundi (Crown of the World). As a tribute to his energy, New York City built a Roerich Museum in 1923 – then the only museum in the United States devoted to the work of a single artist.

Roerich also earned accolades as a humanist, philosopher, explorer, archaeologist and peacemaker. In 1929 he was nominated for the Nobel Peace Prize for his efforts to promote global harmony by "raising the cultural levels of nations . . . and beauty in all spheres of life." His Roerich Peace Pact – an ambitious treaty that sought to preserve cultural monuments from the ravages of war – was supported by the likes of Albert Einstein, H. G. Wells, and George Bernard Shaw.

In all of these endeavors the spirit of Kangchenjunga greatly influenced the Rus-

Japanese painter Katsukyuki Ono proudly displays his painting of Mt. Jannu in the village of Ghunsa. He spent 53 days in the region working on his canvases.

sian scholar. Roerich believed that on the highest mountains "there is the Supreme." And this is what Katsuyuki had tried to capture, and quite successfully I might say, on his dozen canvases.

We ended up staying two days in Ghunsa as the weather flushed itself out. We tried to look up Tharkey, but he was not home. Margie eventually purchased a sheep bell from one of Tharkey's neighbors.

We bade Ghunsa farewell and headed out towards a series of high passes: Sele La, Sinion La and Mirgin La. We hoped the weather would hold. As we ascended the high ridge above Ghunsa, the sun melted the frost so that it dripped in glistening, jewel-like drops from wisps of lichen. A strong wind shredded pillow-shaped cumulus clouds and tossed them like spilled milk across the sky. The bold appearance of lenticulars usually signals a change in the weather. We pressed on.

Despite our two-day rest I felt very tired. My legs felt leaden and my spirit weary. "It's odd that you should feel no energy today," said Pat. "Freshfield felt that way up this pass." The British explorer described his feeling as "a sense of the burden of the body, and a consequent absence of any proper enthusiasm for walking uphill." Less than enthusiastic, I plodded on to our campsite just beyond Sele La. It was already occupied by three small trekking parties. As the latecomers we got the soggiest spot next to a huge pile of trekker's garbage. No one felt much like fraternizing that night.

The view from Sele La has impressed many previous travelers, including Freshfield and Hooker. The latter even called the conical head of Jannu "the most magnificent spectacle I ever beheld." Sella took one of his most compelling images — that of Jannu — near this pass. That photograph remained the trademark portrait of the mountain for decades after. Seventy years later the famous Japanese photographer Yoshikazu Shirakawa planted his tripod at Sele La to produce three images for his over-sized pictorial book, *Himalaya*. Pat headed off with Lhakpa in an effort to produce his own version before night set in. They climbed rapidly for an hour to a ridge crest, but dark clouds obscured everything.

Determined to have a second chance, Pat left an hour before dawn the next day. Although Jannu refused to show its lofty head, several other peaks beamed forth through holes in the gathering clouds. The rest of us broke camp and trudged in ankle-deep snow up the trail to Sinion La at 4740 meters.

A battered garland of prayer flags guarded Sinion La. I walked under them and shouted together with Lhakpa, *"Lha so, so so."* The gods should be thanked.

Margie boogied up the last few steps and broke out into song. "I feel good!" she exclaimed. Both she and Ilana were now well acclimatized and felt jubilant. Jetta, one of our crew, came up last, carrying the case with the oxygen bottle and looking like a goofy doctor out of a Peter Sellers movie. Lhakpa pulled out his packet of chewing tobacco and stuffed a tiny wad behind his lips. "Sherpa altitude medicine," he grinned.

At Sinion La the mountains no longer held our vision hostage. As such the pass provided great vistas and much invigorating sky. To the south, we could see mountains collapsing into gentle waves of foothills as they eventually dissolved into the polluted plains of India. To the west we could see the distinct high summit of Makalu.

We climbed up and down ridges all day long until we came to another high point marked by prayer flags. From this point above the Simbua Khola Valley we had another spectacular view. To the north, the south side of Kangchenjunga held court over the Yalung glacier and the attendant peaks of Kabur and Ratong.

"Look, didi, Kang La," pointed Lale. Straight across to the east we peered into a gently curved valley. Freshfield's party had used this pass to cross back into Sikkim. Traders traditionally chose this high route to reach Darjeeling in order to avoid the malarial jungles of the lowlands.

Not far below us we could hear shrieks of laughter. Three young Israeli trekkers splashed around naked in the icy water of an irresistible tarn on a little plateau. By the time we reached the high alpine bathers, they had regained their composure. They shivered around their little camp stove as they waited for it to brew some strong coffee. "Travelers must not make tea here," Freshfield wrote, "for according to local legend the mountain nymphs who dwell in the water resent its being boiled." We hoped the nymphs would deal gently with the irreverent coffee drinkers.

We slowly descended 1000 vertical knee-jarring meters on a steep switch-backing trail to Tseram. But we had greater ambitions and wanted to reach the viewpoint of Oktang at 4780 meters up the Yalung Valley. From there one could see the whole south face of Kangchenjunga. Margie and Ilana, who felt cheated out of a close-up view of the mountain, were especially keen on this hike. To get there we moved camp north to two stone huts at Ramche.

The snowy path up the Yalung Glacier beyond Ramche followed a narrow defile edged by the lateral moraine. Pat, ever keen to photograph first light, forged ahead with Lhakpa who broke trail in a long stride that belied his height of just over 1.5 meters.

We stopped at Oktang, a place of rock and glacier, and watched as a morning mist unfurled across Kangchenjunga. The sun coming from Sikkim swept the mountain's face. It seemed a fitting place for Ilana to reach her high point. Today was her twenty-first birthday. From here, the mountain looked fierce and inhospitable. But it conjured up fond memories for Lhakpa. His very first job was on this mountain in 1977 with a German expedition.

"I was only the dish boy," recalled Lhakpa. "But when there was no one in camp, it was boring, and I liked to climb. So I went up one small peak with no equipment, using my hands instead of an ice ax. I came down and then went up another one." He showed us the route the Germans had attempted on the south face.

The Yalung Valley had witnessed much interesting climbing history. Aleister Crowley led the first attempt to climb Kangchenjunga from here in 1905. A notori-

A shy Tibetan boy with his mother in Ghunsa. While many of the men in the Himalaya have adopted western garb, women are still wearing traditional clothing such as this colorfully woven apron and silver buckle.

ous rake, who affectionately called himself "the Great Beast," the Briton commanded a small Swiss party that included an Italian hotelier from Darjeeling by the name of de Righi. Midway up the mountain, Crowley got into an argument with the team and retired to his tent. The rest plodded on. Later that day, an avalanche swept away the lead climbers and three Nepali porters. All were killed except for one Swiss and de Righi, who lay half-buried and senseless in the snow. When informed of the mishap Crowley reportedly replied that "a mountain accident of this sort is one of the things for which I have no sympathy whatever." He then added that "the Swiss is old enough to rescue himself, and nobody would want to rescue de Righi."

On his return from Kangchenjunga Crowley stopped off in Darjeeling long enough to indulge in a "brief but intense liaison" with a Nepali girl. Shortly afterwards he absconded with the expedition's remaining funds. Later in his career Crowley chalked up first ascents on the cliffs of Dover that were unrepeated, due to their difficulty, until the 1960s. He also founded the notorious Abbey of Thelema at Celafu in Sicily where he dabbled in debauchery, practiced animal sacrifice and even kept a team of "nuns" as sexual servants. The dissolute climber died an opium addict at the age of 72.

Sunrise from Pangpema.

A British team led by Charles Evans made the first ascent of Kangchenjunga via this southwest face in 1955. There were no Crowley-like fiascos. In due respect to the mountain gods and the wishes of local people, the famous Welsh rock climber Joe Brown and his partner George Band stopped five meters from the top.

After our return to Tseram that afternoon, a festive atmosphere prevailed. Dil baked Ilana a fantastic chocolate birthday cake made with 10 eggs. It read "Happy Birthday Ilana" in white icing. Relieved to be out of the snow zone, the porters wanted to party. I bought them rakshi from the teahouse owner and the singing began. They brought out a two-headed drum called a *maadal* and let their voices lighten up the dark night.

We greatly anticipated our walk up to Kang La the next day. It was an opportunity to feel something of the excitement that Freshfield must have felt while trekking around unknown parts of the mountain for the first time. This valley came with no teahouses and no guidebook descriptions. Nor had any of the AmaDablam staff been up to Kang La. Of course, countless pastoralists and Tibetan traders had come up this valley before us. Upright flat stones, some ancient and some smoke-blackened, stood waiting to become the walls of summer tents. But we strode up the valley in the morning sun as if we had found something new.

By mid-morning we stood at the base of a slope below a narrow rocky notch marked by a cairn. The main valley swept gently to the north. That might have been Freshfield's choice for an ascent and ours as well. We consulted a Nepali map that, at best, was imprecise. But Lhakpa's keen eye told him the notch above would be the most direct route to Sikkim's border. He kicked steps up the slope in shin-deep snow, and within an hour we came to the top and peered into Sikkim.

"Is this your first time in India?," asked Dave.

"Yup," said Lhapka, chuckling with delight.

Looking east we could trace long, undulating ridge lines arching up from the plains. The foothills looked like bony fingers reaching toward the snowy Himalaya. With binoculars we could make out Dzongri, a couple of stone huts on a high plateau. It took Freshfield a day and a half to get there from Kang La. It would take us much longer.

We turned back and glissaded down the snowy pass whooping and hollering. Back on the valley floor we lazed in the warmth of the sun until the mists moved in

Davin Macintosh and Dave Quinn on Mirgin La. The trail to the south base camp of Kangchenjunga runs up the middle of the Yalung Valley far below.

and drove us back to Tseram. Davin bounded ahead of us swigging his protein powder drink that smelled of synthetic banana.

Our trail was now downhill most of the way. Below Tseram, we entered a deep forest, one of the most fantastic Pat and I have ever seen in Nepal. Giant fir trees stood straight and tall with garlands of moss and lichen hanging off the branches. Gray cliffs, mottled with grass and streaks of water, soared above us in this narrow valley. The vibrant display of chlorophyll offered all kinds of wonderful smells. A caravan of five dzopkios from a village in the Kabeli Valley passed us with loads of rice on their way to Ghunsa. A khata was wrapped around the horns of the lead animal and a heavy collar of bells hung from its neck. They clanged and echoed in the stillness as the driver whistled and directed their slow passage upwards. I would have gladly turned around and followed them back up into the highlands.

The next few days became a blur as we descended steep, convoluted hillsides. The mountains seemed to unfold ridge after ridge like an open accordion. In their own way the mountains were slowly flushing us out like silt into rivers. Water buffaloes and cows supplanted high-altitude yaks. I looked back. The snowy peaks, ever shining and tall, looked resplendent.

In the hot climate our grime suddenly became conspicuous. The six of us found a convenient gravel beach by a side creek, concealed from prying eyes. We stripped down and jumped into the cold, refreshing water.

Our group stopped at the first big village, Yamphudin. "Margie is sick in the leg," said Lale, our ever-observant sirdar. Her knees were feeling the torturous descent, even though she was using her ski poles to lessen the impact. We ate outside that night by candlelight. A warm breeze, so calm and soothing, rustled the leaves in the trees. After supper, Margie and the other three played bridge at the table and sipped their alcoholic beverages "like true colonial bastards," as someone put it.

Back in civilization, our porters headed off to find rakshi. The next morning we could smell the alcohol oozing out of them. "Porters are not so good," said Lhakpa. "They spend all their money on drinking." Lhakpa, of course, was no angel himself, nor was Lale who now acted rather subdued. One porter had apparently spent an astronomical sum of 2000 rupees (US$20) on drink for himself and his buddies. It was not uncommon for these young guys to return home penniless by the end of the trek, in spite of a daily wage of 200–250 rupees (US$3.50).

At a place called Sumbi, we camped by a Brahmin's house on a steep hillside etched in terraces. It was our last camp before returning to Khabeli and the road to Birkamod near the Indian border. As we sat and lingered in the warm evening after supper, a six-year-old girl with her hair carefully braided and decorated with red ribbons silently watched us from the terrace above. Davin took a liking to her and stretched out his arms. "Oh, *baihini*. Come here." She then sat on the lap of the big blonde giant who gave her some tea. With her tiny hand clutched to the cup she marveled at the strangeness of bedeshis.

All too soon we heard the grinding of gears and rumbling of a truck as we neared the road. We crossed the bridge over the wide Kabeli Khola and entered a grotty bazaar with the usual shops and a few restaurants. We had to watch our step as garbage lay everywhere. We suddenly realized that our trek had come to an end. After 30 days of following a simple existence in the mountains, we now faced what Nepalis call *jili mili* – the hustle and the bustle.

Almost every climber and explorer experiences mixed feelings at the denouement of a mountain sojourn. It has always been so. The Italian wanderer, Guiseppe

The Tamang porters, Lhakpa Tsering Sherpa (second from right) and our Newari cook Dil (right), formed an integral part of our trekking crew.

126

Tucci, came down from an extended trek in the highlands of Tibet in the 1940s and found the rush of civilization all too maddening:

> For all my tiredness, the thought that we were at the end of our journey struck me as very painful. In a few days we should wallow in the damp heat of Sikkim. Caravan life would be over; we should be speedily carried around by motor cars and railways, locked up into those engine-driven boxes which pitilessly subjected man to the whims of machinery and contrivances. We should no more file out slowly against the outside world, reviewing with attentive, inquisitive eyes the landscape as if we were wresting it every minute from strenuously conquered distances. A treacherous prodigy would make the landscapes whiz along past our windows, blurring their colors and outlines into a dream-like dimness. … Nowadays we are skimming over the surface of things. Machines had accustomed us to see things from afar and at the surface, thus contributing to that lack of depth lamented by the wise ones in our modern age.

So, at the roadhead, where the sound and smell of machines overcame the senses, our journey through Nepal to Kangchenjunga ended. In two days our party would disband at the border and go its separate ways. To mark the end of our trek Dil and the boys butchered two chickens and baked us one last delicious cake. It read "See You Angen (sic)" in red icing letters. The next day we reluctantly piled onto a bus with scabs of rubber peeling off its threadbare tires and drove out of the hills.

Chapter 5

CLOSING THE CIRCLE

Darjeeling, December 1, 1998

PAT, MARGIE AND I LET OUT A COLLECTIVE SIGH OF RELIEF FROM the back seat of our taxi. The sign read, "Darjeeling Police Welcomes You to the Queen of the Hills," and that meant we had to be close to tea town. It had been a long journey. In fact it had taken us ten days by foot, bus and taxi to reach a point where we could legally cross into India from the remote hills of southeastern Nepal.

We directed our taxi to the upper end of the town to a pedestrian plaza known as the Mall and searched for a place to stay. In the square, horse wallahs offered rides on their bony steeds and a couple of kids played hackey sack with a Barbie doll's head. Darjeeling still looked dowdy, but the December sun brightened the old colonial town.

We found a quaintly ramshackle hotel close by run by a smiling Tibetan named Karma. He wore thick glasses and an imitation Patagonia fleece jacket. While thumbing prayer beads he gamboled up the creaky wooden stairs of the Main Bellevue Hotel to show us a spacious room for three. It contained a boarded-up fireplace, a worn-out sofa, a few reading chairs, and cheap paintings of palm trees. It looked like a good place to drink gin and tonics in true British style and rest

The rising sun casts golden light over Kangchenjunga and the
frosted prayer flags on top of Dzongri Peak in Sikkim.

for five days before embarking on one more trek to "Kang" as we now called "our" mountain.

Karma drew back the curtains on a side window and said, "And look, there you will see Kangchenjunga in the morning when it is clear. This room has best view."

Winter is off-season in Darjeeling and most hotels such as the Main Bellevue offer a discount rate. "Price good: 650 rupees, three people. Bed tea also coming in that price," said Karma. That translated to US$16 a night. A slightly more upscale room at the elegant Windamere Hotel, where jazz bands once entertained wealthy patrons, went for more than five times that.

We still owed our taxi driver money and we asked Karma if he could change our travelers checks. He said that he could not. But he then pulled 1,500 rupees out of his pocket and handed the wad to me. "Here, you pay me back later, okay?" With this simple gesture, he sealed our trust and friendship. We paid the driver, settled into our room and ordered a pot of tea.

True to Karma's word, Kangchenjunga floated into view the next morning. We headed out for Observatory Hill, just as we had last April, to pay tribute to "The Five Treasuries of Eternal Snow." This time we found a hilltop shrine littered with the wilted petals of marigold flowers. One never needs much of an excuse for worship in this part of the world.

Each morning we walked to Glenary's, an eatery that first opened in 1935. It served Darjeeling's famous tea in brass teapots together with an excellent Indian version of croissants. Pat took part in his version of the "Great Game" which was to try to find a real cup of coffee on the Indian subcontinent. He settled, as usual, for a pot of instant Nescafe.

We now waited for three Canadian friends in their early forties who would help us finish our circuit of Kangchenjunga. The first two, Karen Barkley and Jill Keifer, arrived by plane and taxi. We had not seen Karen since early summer and she quickly fueled our evening conversations with tales of a five-month journey in Tibet and Nepal. Jill, who was on the rebound from a wavering long-distance love affair, had come to India to find her heart again. A third friend, Frances Klatzel, now living and working in Kathmandu, promised to meet us in Gangtok.

The peaceful garden of the Main Bellevue Hotel became our haven. We did not feel any need to cram our days with sight-seeing with one important exception, the gompa in nearby Ghoom. Earlier in the century it had been the home of a famous Buddhist scholar with an unusual past.

Ernst Lothar Hoffman, known to the world as Lama Anagarika Govinda, grew up in Germany. The young man's interest in philosophy and religion led him initially to Buddhist monasteries in Sri Lanka (then Ceylon), and finally India. In 1929, he came to Darjeeling and found, or was found by, a great Guru named Tomo Geshe Rinpoche at the Yigah Chöling gompa.

The Tibetan abbot became the German's life-long teacher and inspired him to follow the Tantric path of Buddhism. His search for eternal truths took him into Sikkim where he visited the same lama that coached Alexandra David-Neel. To earn a living the German briefly taught languages at a college near Calcutta. One of his young French students eventually became India's first female prime minister, Indira Gandhi.

The ever-humble Govinda never wavered from his chosen path. Before his death in 1985 the learned scholar had become something of a guru himself. During the 1960s Beat poets such as Gary Snyder and Allen Ginsberg sought out the lama, as did the American writer Peter Matthiessen. Govinda's best-known book, *The Way of the White Clouds,* remains one of the most popular interpretations of Buddhist thought ever written.

The monastery at Ghoom, where Lama Govinda absorbed the dharma, or teachings, lies eight kilometers south of Darjeeling. The best way to get there is by a famous but very slow, toy train. Completed in 1881 the narrow-gauge railway originally served the tea plantations. We bought tickets for 3 rupees or 8 cents and squeezed onto narrow wooden benches along with a Calcutta family bundled in woolen hats and sweaters.

A shrill whistle signaled the train's departure and we rattled slowly down the winding tracks. Black coal smoke poured though open windows and coated passengers with a sooty grime.

We arrived at Ghoom's station almost 30 minutes later, having traveled at a belabored rate of one kilometer every four minutes. We walked through a grotty bazaar and found our way to the gompa. Wires from a generating station hummed with electricity between tall steel towers. A file of graying prayer flags on slender bamboo poles lined the pathway and seemingly rippled with a different energy.

The Yigah Chöling gompa is a dirty-white concrete structure with colorful dragons painted above its entrance. Its main treasure is an important statue of Maitreya, the Buddha of the Future. Unlike most lotus-positioned Buddhas, the blue-eyed Maitreya is depicted with his feet on the ground as if ready to arise and walk in the modern world. Buddhists believe that Maitreya will appear 30,000 years from now.

I walked up above the monastery onto the wooded hillside. The mist brushed my cheek and tugged at the curtains of faded prayer flags draped in the trees. Hidden in the copse was a hermitage, a small one-roomed structure, now locked. Perhaps Lama Govinda had meditated there. I wondered how the monks could find silence and peace when so many noisy camera-happy tourists, Indians and foreigners alike, bustled through their prayer hall. An endless stream of vehicles on the nearby road also disturbed the silent sanctity of the place.

Back in Darjeeling we made plans to get to Gangtok. Rather than take a bus, we hired a Land Rover and driver. Karma introduced us to the vehicle's owner, a one-armed Bengali.

"You are the driver?" I asked somewhat amused.

"No, no," he laughed. "I will send you another driver. But do not misjudge my driving abilities just because I have only one arm. I can show you my driving certificate and letters of appreciation from tourists." A young two-armed Sherpa delivered us to Gangtok, unscathed.

Except for mercifully cooler temperatures, Gangtok remained the same since our last visit: a center of frenzied construction. Laborers worked into the night chipping away at the street right next to our hotel. The endless wheel of development had found another home in Gangtok.

The manager of the Hotel Sonam Delek ("proudly Sikkimese, built and managed by local people," claimed its brochure) was clearly a Bengali from India's hot plains. He huddled behind the reception desk, slapping his arms against his sides to stay warm. "Welcome, how long will you stay?" Tourist traffic was down at this time of year.

"Two nights. Our friend is coming tomorrow from Kathmandu. Then we will leave the day after," I replied.

He exhaled a disappointed sigh. "But will you eat in our restaurant?" he pleaded. The hotel's restaurant had unfortunately been named The Oyster. Here in a land-locked state, hundreds of kilometers from the ocean, it did not sound very appealing.

"We will probably go out," answered Pat, remembering the tasty momos we had enjoyed at the Hotel Tibet down the way.

Our hotel room had cable TV and later that evening, we sat glued to the tube, like moths attracted to light. During any trip of long duration both wondrous and calamitous events are bound to happen. When Freshfield and company returned to Darjeeling in 1899 they learned that the Boer War had just broken out. Now, we watched in disbelief as American and British warplanes mercilessly bombed Iraq.

Frances Klatzel arrived very late the next evening after we had all long gone to bed. Her journey from Kathmandu to Gangtok had turned into an eventful succession of plane and taxi delays. In India a "greasy customs agent" stepped onto the road, stopped her taxi and pawed through everyone's belongings looking for smuggled Nepali goods. The vehicle later broke down in the jungle in the middle of the night.

"To top it all off, when I got out of the car, I stepped right smack into a pile of shit," Frances groaned, as she stood in her bare feet the next morning. "Luckily, I got a ride from a van, and it all ended up OK but my runners are still drying in the bathroom. It's great to see you guys."

We had already met our amiable trek organizer, Norbu Bhutia. He was part owner of Denzong Adventure Mountaineering and Trekking. Norbu had set up a standard 10-day itinerary to Dzongri, a high alpine ridge in the lower reaches of southern Kangchenjunga. Until recently the government of India only allowed tourists to visit Dzongri or the area around Gangtok. Both places are far away from the sensitive border with Tibet and China. Nevertheless foreigners must still hire an agency to go trekking.

Our six-hour drive west to Yuksam, the starting point of our trek, was longer than advertised. The clutch cable on Norbu's Land Rover needed a quick repair. We waited for an hour on the outskirts of Gangtok. Finally Norbu muttered, "God bless us," and flashed a winning smile as he started the Land Rover again. Norbu now brought along a teenaged assistant armed with a pair of pliers and a twist of haywire in case of further breakdowns.

We arrived at Yuksam in the dark and waited til morning to explore. The village, a cluster of houses on a wooded knoll, is the historic "meeting place of the three superior ones." In 1642 three Tibetan lamas assembled at this hill to consecrate Sikkim's first King, Phuntsog Namgyal — a dynasty that lasted more than 300 years.

The corduroy trail up to the Dzongri Trekker's Hut passes through an old-growth rhododendron and fir forest.

An ancient stone throne and *chorten*, a Buddhist monument, decorated with strings of prayer flags still mark the spot.

One of the three superior lamas, Lhatsun Chempo, brought Buddhism to Sikkim. Also known as Lhatsun Namkhe Jigme or "the Reverend God who fears not the sky," this lama possessed extraordinary abilities that allowed him to fly. From the summit of Mount Kabru he found a hidden paradise or bayul just south of Kangchenjunga. Locating such a magical and powerful place is not easy. It takes great mental clarity and sound spirit. Yet the most secret sanctum, allegedly concealed within the deep embrace of Kangchenjunga, still awaits discovery.

The search for this bayul continues to this day. In 1975 the lama, Tulshok Lingba, started walking towards Kangchenjunga with a group of followers to find and celebrate the sacred sanctuary. Prophesy did not favor Tulshok's quest and somewhere along the way, he fell off a cliff and died. His followers, many from Yuksam, had great difficulty returning. Some also perished along the way.

When I awoke at No. 1 Forest Guest House the next morning the mountains did not reveal any immediate secrets. A haphazard assembly of houses and fields sprawled across the hill-top plateau while the Rathong River dug its course through the valley several hundred meters below us. But try as I might, my untrained eyes saw no signs of anything sacred. Nor had Sir Joseph Hooker nearly 150 years ago. The British explorer simply described Yuksam as "the most level area I know of in Sikkim." For a largely vertical country dominated by hills, Hooker's description remains quite a statement.

But Yuksam has a newer claim to fame – a garish pink concrete three-star hotel, called the Tashi Gang. It stood out like a baboon's rear end according to Pat. It is the legacy of Yuksam's prodigal son, Danny Denzong, now one of the most popular Hindi film stars in all of India. The hotel's gaping satellite dish pointed heavenward in a presumptuous gesture of collecting and dispensing the wisdom of our age. It certainly wasn't the magic others had sought in these mountains.

In Sikkim the truest believers are the Lepchas, an indigenous people. One of the last remaining pockets of these gentle forest people lives near Yuksam. To Freshfield "their eyes seemed to have seen all the mysteries of the woods." The Lepchas, which now make up only 18 percent of Sikkim's population, call their home Mayel Lyang, "the land of hidden paradise or the delightful abode."

According to their legends the world's very first people emerged from the womb of great Kangchenjunga. Lepcha scholar K. P. Tamsang, who died in Gangtok in 1985, wrote passionately about his people in *The Unknown and Untold Reality about the Lepchas*. The scholar explained that "Sikkim is located right here on the very sacred lap of the holy and the mighty Kangchenjunga, at the intersection of the east, west, north and south, that is, the real and actual center, or the focal point of the universe."

The Lepchas, however, are no longer at the center of this universe. During his trek Freshfield often lamented how these people were "being gradually supplanted by the masterful Nepalese, a race of far greater force of character and appreciation of material advantages. The district is, for better, for worse, rapidly becoming Nepalised."

Later that morning we met a real Lepcha.

"My name is Lhatsun Lepcha," said the handsome young man. (Lepchas, like all hill people, adopt their tribal names as surnames.)

"Oh, like Lhatsun Chempo?" I asked. He seemed pleased to be compared to Sikkim's legendary founder. "Yes, it is a popular name. I am proud to be a Lepcha." He spoke good English and explained that he was on his way to a special celebration that night in the nearby shaman's house. He wore a knee-length tunic of colorful striped woven fabric and a cap shaped like that of a Chinese mandarin.

Our sirdar on the Dzongri trek was 24-year-old Dawa Tamang. In spite of his youth he had walked the trail 25 times. The young man was even more soft-spoken than his boss Norbu, yet eager to answer any questions about himself and his home.

His father, the head lama of Temi, had expected his son to become a monk. After a few years of attending a monastic school in Gangtok, Dawa quit, creating tension in the family. "But when I started to give my family some money that I earned from trekking, they accepted my wishes." In the off-season he still helps in the family fields, where they grow cash crops such as ginger and cardamom, and important staples such as potatoes, cabbages and cauliflowers.

In addition to Dawa our group included a cook, two Sherpas from Nepal and three porters from Yuksam who carried our gear on four dzopkios. On the outskirts of the village we came across an unlikely colony of concrete houses arranged in well-managed rows in a flat cleared area. At first we mistook the buildings for some kind of resort development. In fact, the ghost town proved to be the remains of the ill-planned Rathong Khola hydroelectric project. Pressure from Indian environmentalists and Sikkimese monks forced the government to abandon the boondoggle in 1995. Yuksam is considered holy land; even the great Buddhist sage and footprint maker, Guru Rinpoche, had hidden special treasures in the area. Dawa told us the buildings would now house a monastic college.

The Dzongri trail led us northward into the deep furrow of a gorge. The rich canopy of trees that rose up from the crystalline waters of the Rathong River drew us back a century. Freshfield described these old forests as "sylvan" and rightly so. Towering chestnut, oak and deodar (cedar) trees kept us sheltered from the hot December sun as we slowly gained elevation. There was only one village beyond Yuksam.

That night we camped on a patch of well-trampled grass in the tiny village of Tsoka. Nearly 35 years ago the King of Sikkim gave the land and extensive alpine grazing rights to some Tibetan refugees. According to Dawa, the King "wanted his yaks taken care of." As the villagers established themselves they gradually cut down or pruned most of the immediate forest for fuel or shelter.

Now, a non-governmental organization, The Mountain Institute in West Virginia, was working with the locals to promote environmental conservation standards and solid ecotourism practices. As a result of their efforts, local revenues from trekking tourism have increased by 25 percent while fuel wood use among tourism operators, their staff and porters, has decreased by more than 25 percent. Local crews kept the path well maintained and rubble-free. Government money also supported a well-constructed Trekker's Hut with several spartan rooms, cooking space and a large central area. It even had clean latrines and a cement water reservoir with a spigot.

As darkness and fog engulfed the village, we headed out on a thomba hunt. I was keen to indoctrinate Karen and Jill into the drink's popular society and they were willing subjects. We picked our way along the narrow muddy trail between the fenced yards. Dim fluorescent light beamed from three lampposts charged by solar panels that had been installed by the government in 1996. Each house also had a panel on its roof.

A kindly old Tibetan woman with sight in only one eye welcomed us into her house. She had earlier tried to sell us yak wool hats. Charmed by her motherly manner, we called her Ama-la. As she fussed with boiling water and rinsed the thomba containers, we reveled in the warm glow of the wood fire. The small kitchen was just big enough to sit all of us on wide benches that served as beds. The cool radiance of a fluorescent bulb suffused the room. On one wall, a plain altar with seven bowls of water tended to the gods.

Like most of her kinfolk, Ama-la lived alone during grazing season. Her husband was now herding a few head of yak up at Dzongri, and would soon be bringing them down for the winter. Her adult children lived elsewhere, mostly in Darjeeling. Ama-la and her husband had come from Tibet, from Yuthang in the Chumbi Valley, in the early 1960s.

"Have you been to Tibet?" she asked in Nepali. "*Char manche.*" Yes, four of us, replied Frances.

"Oh, thank you," Ama-la replied in her few words of English. She made us feel as though we had done her and Tibet a great favor. As a displaced person she knew that Tibet's eventual freedom from Chinese oppression depended on more people caring about her beleaguered country.

The Tibetan's cheerful character more than compensated for her slightly moldy tasting thomba. As we sipped the grog the woman took advantage of her captive audience and made a sales pitch. With the guarded movement of arthritic hands she unwrapped a dirty cloth that held pieces of turquoise, prayer beads made of Tibetan juniper berries and a bell. She also showed us an antique chang cup. "Very old," she said. Frances took a liking to a well-crafted, nine-eyed *zee* stone slung on a string. Of mysterious origin, authentic zees can bring good luck to their wearers. It was most likely a fake since real ones can cost hundreds of dollars. But Frances was willing to take a chance. Before draping it around her neck the next morning, she passed it back and forth over the smoke of a juniper fire. This purification ritual "cleansed the karma" of the stone's previous owner.

During the monsoon season Dzongri gets a terrific amount of rain. A corduroy staircase made of thick logs laid sideways had been built to preserve the trail beyond Tsoka. The morning's sunshine was soon obliterated by a wave of cold fog that spilt over the landscape. We plodded up the steep ridge. The weather encouraged inward thoughts. Beyond the easy reach of the villagers, giant firs now graced the trail with their ghostly silhouettes. Long strands of lichen moved in the current of the silent fog.

We passed a couple of fenced-off experimental plots that had been placed by The Mountain Institute to measure the impact of livestock grazing. In the protected area grew a luxuriant bed of grasses and other low slung plants. Outside it yaks and other animals had chewed everything down to bald turf.

The fog brought a cold wind and the dzopkios' feet skidded on the icy trail. We arrived at the deserted Dzongri Trekker's Hut in a total whiteout. We found the caretaker in a dark room seated beside a companion and a puppy dog around a dwindling fire. He had planned to leave that afternoon but we convinced him to give us the key so we could use the main room to eat in. We prepared for a cold night. Dawa assured us that the sky would clear by morning and that our hike up to 4300-meter-high Dzongri Peak would give us a splendid viewpoint.

The scraping sound of light falling snow on the tent walls lulled me to sleep. As predicted, the clouds lifted. At 4:30 A.M. we quaffed bed tea and stumbled out into the starlight. There was enough light in the expiring moon to illuminate our way up the peak. Our boots crunched in a thin crisp skin of snow which made footing slightly treacherous on the steep hogs backed ridge. My legs brushed against the aromatic rubbery leaves of alpine rhododendron, a plant locals use as sweet-smelling incense. After an hour we reached the top well before first light.

Morning mist swirls around Rumtek, one of Sikkim's most famous monasteries, 24 kilometers from Gangtok.

In the fading darkness one of our Sherpas pointed out the distant lights of Darjeeling. Just a week ago we had gazed admiringly at Kangchenjunga from tea town's Observatory Hill. Now, in the southern lap of the mountain, we stared back at the lights of the city. To the west we could make out Kang La on the border with Nepal. A trek to Dzongri would have taken little more than a day's walk from there. Instead we had spent two weeks going the round about way as government protocol demanded.

The sun first illuminated Kangchenjunga's main summit. Pink light followed and glowed fiercely on the white snow and ice. Kangchenjunga was in the best of tempers. The light danced over to the white crest of Mount Pandim and licked its face until it also flushed a rosy color. To the west, the double snow peaks of Kabru shimmered. Finally, the sun crept over Tenzing Kang and Narsing, bare rock peaks that form the backbone of an intervening ridge to the east. The sun began to thaw our freezing limbs. It was a splendid morning.

Every August the monks from Pemayangtse Monastery in Pelling come here to give a puja to the god of Kangchenjunga. The peak made a suitably inspiring place for prayer and offerings. Nearby there was also a place called De-chhen phu, or the "Cave of Great Happiness." It was one of the four great caves of Sikkim hallowed as the traditional abodes of two of the region's most famous and magical lamas, Guru Rinpoche and Lhatsun Chempo.

In our own time, we slowly wandered back down the hill. Along the way Frances and Jill met a Tibetan monk in a large meadow dotted with a few stone huts for herders. Dressed in a bare armed robe and flip-flops, he had come out to fetch water. As a Sherpa translated, the monk told them he was from Sera Monastery in south India. He had come to this lonely place three months ago to do a five-year retreat. When he learned that the visitors were from Canada, he became very excited because his guru was now living there. Maybe they could bring back a letter for him, he asked. After some thought Frances agreed to give it a try (Canada, after all, is a big place) and the monk hastily wrote a note.

Overnight it snowed again – enough to top our boots. The clouds pressed low to the ground as if trying to smother us. We discussed what to do. Jill, whose face had puffed up due to the altitude, had slept poorly that night. We had no desire to soldier off into oblivion with or without a sick team member in tow. We made the decision to forgo the remaining two-day round trip hike to Goecha La.

The monks of Rumtek Monastery perform the sacred Kagyat dances on the 28th and 29th days of the 10th month according to the Buddhist calendar (in December).

For Freshfield and Sella that 4940-meter pass marked the last high point of their circuit of Kangchenjunga before returning to Darjeeling. Freshfield, then an agile 54 years of age, recalled his arrival in the British city with typical aplomb:

> One more canter, and I found myself, thanks to my excellent pony, a little ahead of my companions, on 'the Mall.' A respectable Babu addressed me – 'Pardon me, sir, taking liberty, but are you one of the party from the Snows? Looking at appearances, I presume it probable.' When I informed him that he was not mistaken in the inference he drew from my burnt face, blistered lips, and generally battered appearance, he responded, with the remark, 'What courage, above all at your advanced years!' Highly flattered, I pushed on, and a few minutes later alighted before the hospitable door from which we had started for the Tour of Kangchenjunga, and found myself welcomed, an incongruous object, at an elegant tea-table.

Freshfield's love for the mountains never abated. After the trek he later became president of the prestigious Royal Geographical Society. And when his active climb-

The view of Tibet across the Sikkim Himalaya from the slopes of Mt. Siniolchu.

ing career ended in 1920, he continued to visit the mountains by car, driven by a faithful chauffeur. Inevitably, the steepest and highest roads were always chosen. When the explorer died at the age of 89 his peers paid homage to "a great and very perfect gentleman, peerless mountain explorer, wise counselor, patriot and friend – one who stood so far above us all."

After Kangchenjunga the master photographer Vittorio Sella continued to profile alpine subjects. In 1906 he accompanied the Duke of Abruzzi to the Ruwenzori mountains of Africa, and later to the Karakoram, where he created the single finest representation of a mountain range ever undertaken. But Freshfield always contended that Sella never "worked with more uniform success than under the shadow of the highest Himalaya."

Our circuit of Kangchenjunga which had taken two trips, and more than three months, now came to an end. As we descended from Dzongri our snowy beasts of burden, the dzopkios, shook their heads with a clanging of bells. We watched a herder invoking the gods over a fire of green juniper branches. Perhaps this puja was meant for us as well. The flames crackled and sputtered as the thick smoke sanctified the muted, gray day.

At the far end of the Dzongri ridge, the trail dramatically plummeted down into the Rathong Valley. Strings of prayer flags now touched us with their wind-swept blessings. I looked back up the valley toward Kangchenjunga to "another and less material world" as Freshfield wrote, where our footsteps disappeared into the clouds.

VITTORIO SELLA:
THE ALPINE MASTER

by Pat Morrow

I BECAME AN INSTANT ADMIRER OF VITTORIO SELLA 25 YEARS AGO WHEN I came across a lithographed collection of his black-and-white images from the Himalaya and Alaska. At the time I had just entered the rarefied world of freelance photography, and I wanted to specialize in alpine adventures. Sella's work set a new standard for me.

The great mountain photographer was born in the town of Biella at the foot of the Italian Alps in 1859. Originally trained as a chemist to work at his family's textile-manufacturing company, Sella became a photographer instead and traveled the world. He spent the first 10 years of his career photographing the Alps in the company of his brothers, including Erminio (who would also accompany him in the Caucasus and Sikkim). In 1889, 1890 and 1896 Vittorio journeyed to the Caucasus of Russia and collaborated with Douglas Freshfield on a handsome two-volume book set. He then began to document a series of remarkable climbing expeditions to Alaska, Sikkim, the Karakorum and Africa. His photographs of alpine landscapes in these regions are still some of the finest representations of mountain ranges ever done. He remained an active alpinist, in spirit at least, until his death in 1943.

Before discovering Sella, I had held the American Ansel Adams in highest esteem. Early in this century Adams gracefully took the photographic baton from

Although burdened by his heavy camera equiptment, Sella always made great efforts to find the right angle for his mountain images, such as this one of Jannu in Nepal. PHOTO: VITTORIO SELLA

Sella and sprinted into prominence with black-and-white landscapes that shimmered with all the life that silver halides suspended in a layer of gelatin can possibly possess. But unlike the adventurous Sella (the Italian made the first winter ascent of the Matterhorn, among other mountaineering accomplishments), Adams was not a climber. In fact, he shot his best landscapes of the American West from a platform he built upon the roof of his International Harvester Travelall truck. Sella, on the other hand, performed his magic on foot in the most remote corners of the globe.

In Sella's day photography required enormous patience and skill to render an image. Before 1879 Sella prepared wet collodion film emulsions on glass plates in the field. Just three years later commercially prepared dry plates became available. Whereas Adams based his zone system of light measurement on a highly accurate light meter, Sella did not even own one. Exposures were a matter of trial-and-error and required a tacit understanding of light and photo-sensitive materials.

These technical hurdles make Sella's achievements in photography all the more formidable. Adams recognized that: "Sella has brought to us not only the facts and forms of far-off splendors, but the essence of experience which finds a spiritual response in the inner recesses of our mind and heart."

In the fall of 1998 I made a pilgrimage to Sella's hometown of Biella at the foot of the Italian Alps, where his descendants have created the Institute for Alpine Photography now under the auspices of Fondazione Sella-Biella. It is housed in former offices of the family's textile business. My friendly hosts were Lodovico Sella, a banker and an adventurer with a personal interest in his great uncle's work, and his gracious wife Alessandra.

According to Lodovico, Sella became a full-time photographer thanks to a near-fatal accident. On his way to give a lecture at the Royal Geographical Society in England the seasoned alpinist stuck his head out a train window to admire the view and cracked his skull at the edge of a tunnel entrance.

"Something good came out of it because the insurance money gave him enough support during convalescence to develop his lifetime career of selling prints," explained Lodovico.

Lodovico led me on a tour of his great uncle's legacy, beginning with Sella's darkroom, which is located on the upper floor of a now-vacant house. At the center of the workplace stands a floor-to-ceiling solar enlarger for the smaller negatives from his hand-held cameras. A hole in the roof of the house admits the light, which streams through the negative in the enlarger and exposes the paper.

With his training as a chemist, Sella was as adept at manipulating images in the darkroom as he was at gathering them in the field. As far back as 1900, Sella's printing skills went beyond simple burning and dodging, the common techniques for enhancement of light and dark portions of the print. By creating and overlaying neutral-density masks he could greatly reduce the contrast on some of his problem negatives. He even went so far as to "sandwich" negatives in order to create composites, a procedure that took hours and even days to complete. Nowadays, with the advent of digital imaging, these effects can be accomplished with the flick of a computer mouse.

At the behest of the institute, darkroom technician Luciano Pivotto has spent several years restoring Sella's original glass and film negatives. Measuring up to 46 × 56 cm, the plates were stored in wooden boxes that Sella built. These large plates captured a range of detail that is now impossible to render on 35 mm film – the most popular format being used today.

Sella's favorite instruments were cumbersome Dallmeyer and Ross view cameras, which were about the size of a scaled-down IMAX movie camera. Even with assistance from his porters, it is hard to imagine Sella hauling the wooden-bodied cameras, plus tripod and glass plates, across glaciers and high passes, let alone struggling to set up the camera in high winds.

The Italian master favored large format prints, but he also made stereoscopic photos (for use with a stereoscopic viewer), telephotos (some of his most effective images) and panoramas that were really several photos pasted side by side. A folding Kodak rollfilm camera allowed him the portability of a modern 35 mm camera. But he liked large format because of its superior ability to amass detail.

For the Kangchenjunga trip Sella could not bring much film material because of its weight and bulkiness. On our circuit, I shot maybe 150 36-exposure rolls, while Sella managed just 196 - 20 × 25 cm plates and a small collection of stereo photos. The difference between our shooting styles is dramatic. While he was forced to consider each composition seriously before he even set up his tripod (an exercise that took several minutes), I could snap off a few frames in seconds.

The weight of my two 35 mm camera bodies and three or four lenses plus film was much less than the steamer trunk Sella used to ship his equipment to India. The combination of light-sensitive, high-speed film and image-stabilizer lenses allowed me to handhold many of my shots, even with telephoto lenses. Sella shot everything from a heavy tripod.

While leafing through his contact prints from Kangchenjunga, it became apparent that Sella had little interest in documenting the European members of his party. He only placed them in his photographs to help measure scale. On the other hand,

*Lodovico Sella, with his great uncle Vittorio's favorite large format camera
at the Fondazione Sella in Biella, Italy.*

his photos of porters and holy men were somewhat more intimate. Sella lovingly chronicled the everyday life and religious customs of Himalaya natives. And even though he was photographing in black and white, a good portion of his shots interpreted the local flora.

In addition to being an author, Sella's companion Douglas Freshfield was also a critic of photography. In 1894 he made a prophetic observation about the now popular business of putting the mountain experience into books and on film:

> Mountaineers are sometimes charged with making the most of their gymnastic feats. Those I have known have been for the most part modest and precise, not to say prosaic persons – at any rate in their writings. But I cannot claim as much for their cameras. These little instruments are given to sensationalism of the crudest kinds. They make the easiest rocks look highly dangerous, and difficult cliffs impossible. Let wives and mothers take heart – mountaineering is not nearly so bad as it is photographed.

Sella never made that mistake.

Compilations of Sella's work appear, with Italian text, in the following books:

Dal Caucaso Al Himalaya 1889-1909 – Vittorio Sella fotografo alpinista esploratore. Torino: Touring Club Italiano/Club Alpino Italiano, 1981.

Vittorio Sella – Fotografie e Montagna Nell' Ottocento. Torino: Priuli & Verlucca, editori, Museo Nazionale della Montagna "Duca degli Abruzzi," 1982.

"Vittorio Sella," *Alpinismo*. Carlo Ramella, Annuario del Club Alpino Accademico Italiano, n. 94, 1992, biographical essay pp. 33-49.

Sources in English:

Kallmes, Paul. *Summit: Vittorio Sella, Mountaineer and Photographer: The Years 1879–1909*. New York, NY: Aperture Books, 1999.

Bensen, Joe. *Souvenirs From High Places: A History of Mountaineering Photography*. Seattle: The Mountaineers, 1998.

Selected Reading

Bauer, Paul. *Himalayan Quest*. London: Nicholson and Watson, 1938.

Bedi, Rajesh. *Sikkim*. New Delhi: Brijbasi Printers, 1989.

Bernbaum, Edwin. *Sacred Mountains of the World*. San Francisco: Sierra Club Books, 1990.

Bezruchka, Stephen. *Trekking in Nepal: A Traveler's Guide*. Seattle: The Mountaineers, 1997.

Crossette, Barbara. *So Close to Heaven: The Vanishing Buddhist Kingdoms of the Himalayas*. New York: Alfred A. Knopf, 1995.

Datta-Ray, Sunanda K. *Smash and Grab: The Annexation of Sikkim*. Delhi: Vikas Publishing House, 1984.

David-Neel, Alexandra. *Magic and Mystery in Tibet*. London: Unwin, 1965.

Freshfield, Douglas. *Round Kangchenjunga: A Narrative of Mountain Travel and Exploration*. London: Edward Arnold, publisher to HM India Office, 1903. (reprint 1979) Kathmandu: Ratna Pustak Bhandar.

Govinda, Anagarika Govinda. *The Way of the White Clouds – A Buddhist in Tibet*. Lama Ms Rider & Co., 1960.

Himalayan Journals, or Notes of a Naturalist in Bengal, the Sikkim and Nepal Himalayas and the Khasia Mountains. London: J. D. Hooker, 1854.

Smythe, Frank. *The Kangchenjunga Adventure*. London: Victor Gollancz, 1930.

Tamsang, K. P. *Lepchas: The Unknown and Untold Reality about the Lepchas*. Kalimpong, India: Mani Printing Press, 1983/98.

Waddell, L. A. *Among the Himalayas*. Delhi: Pilgrims Book, 1998.

A religious ceremony at Chungthang. PHOTO: VITTORIO SELLA

Acknowledgments

It is one thing to have a dream. It is quite another to find the means to make that dream come true. We could never have brought this project to fruition without the unflagging support of family, friends and associates. In particular, many thanks go to two organizations that offer grant programs to seat-of-the-pants adventurers like ourselves: Malden Mills, who proffer the *Polartec Challenge Award* (administered by the enthusiastic Ruthann Brown) and the Banff Centre for Mountain Culture, steered by Bernadette Macdonald. With their generous financial support we were able to cover the huge costs for the Mount Siniolchu expedition.

Numerous individuals and companies provided their high-quality services, products and assistance. A special thanks goes to Ravi Chandra at AmaDablam Adventure Group in Kathmandu. Others who helped out with the logistics include Karma and Wendy Lama at Cho Oyu Trekking in Kathmandu; Norbu Lama at Denzong Adventure Mountaineering & Trekking in Gangtok; Jamling Tenzing of Tenzing Norgay Adventures in Darjeeling; and Kandy Akina in the Los Angeles office of Singapore Airlines. Thanks also to the purveyors of excellent products: Sandro Parisotto, Scarpa; Allen Slade, Patagonia; Peter Kruka, Agfa; Michael Mayzel, Daymen Photo Marketing; Jim Lyon, Kodak; Gioachino and Betta Gobbi, Grivel; Ted Allsop, Extreme Optiks; Gramicci; Clif Bar; Gregory Mountain Products; and Marmot Mountain Ltd.

Molte grazie to Mr. and Mrs. Lodovico Sella at Fondazione Sella in Biella, Italy, who hosted Pat in September 1998. Lodovico provided personal insight into Vittorio Sella's photography and gave us permission to use some of his work.

We are always humbled by the generosity of the mountain people. Lhakpa Tsering Sherpa, Nima Norbu, Pasang, Temba, Sangay, Ugen Bhutia, Dorjee Lhatoo, Lal Bahadur, Manish Suba, Dil and Dawa Tamang showed us around their magnificent back yard. Our fun-loving *bedeshi* companions on the two trips provided the fodder for the story.

Raincoast Books showed their own adventurous side when Mark Stanton invited us to submit the proposal. Brian Scrivener gave us the vote of confidence to proceed and nurtured the book to its conclusion. Paul Kallmes, Joe Bensen, Tony Leighton, Bruce Morrison, Frances Klatzel and Stephen Bezruchka offered much appreciated input into the manuscript, and word wizard Andrew Nikiforuk took it to a higher level.

Finally, heartfelt thanks to Francie Cochran and Debbie Senger for tending the home fires and keeping our insatiable jade plant alive.